Britain's Cities, Britain's Future

T0154669

PERSPECTIVES

Series editor: Diane Coyle

Britain's Cities, Britain's Future

Mike Emmerich

Copyright © 2017 Mike Emmerich

Published by London Publishing Partnership
www.londonpublishingpartnership.co.uk

Published in association with
Enlightenment Economics
www.enlightenmenteconomics.com

All Rights Reserved

ISBN: 978-1-907994-62-3 (pbk)

A catalogue record for this book is
available from the British Library

This book has been composed in Candara

Copy-edited and typeset by
T&T Productions Ltd, London
www.tandtproductions.com

This book is dedicated to those lost to the long process of urban industrial decline in Britain

Contents

Preface

I grew up on a council estate in Manchester and left school in 1982 as the city hit rock bottom. My working life since then has been spent in think tanks, at HM Treasury, and as a senior adviser in the Number 10 Policy Unit. Much of my work has been on cities, local government and what the government likes to call 'local growth'. In a move many civil servants might term brave, I eventually returned to Manchester, initially to the university before spending nine years as the first chief executive of New Economy. This organization has been described by the *Financial Times* as 'Manchester's brain trust' and had a central role in the development of Greater Manchester's approach to its economy and devolution.[1] Now, at my own business, Metro Dynamics, my colleagues and I work with cities across and beyond the UK. These three decades of experience – watching the games of politics and policy at close quarters – inform this book, as does the literature on the economics, history and geography of urban Britain.

Devolution has been the focus of a sizeable part of my working life of late. But this book isn't about how Howard Bernstein and I, with others, navigated a path through Whitehall to get some real power for Manchester. Instead it looks more broadly at the current wave of devolution, the renaissance of cities that is underway, and at the rises and falls in the economic and political power of cities that preceded them. More importantly, it looks at where Britain goes next. This is the most significant period for our cities, and our nation, since World War II, and that has only been made more true by Britain's decision to leave the European Union. The Brexit vote has prompted a national existential debate, but our cities have been undergoing this for some time. Even London, which has been so confident about its place in the world elite, now needs to consider its global role. This book considers some of the ways in which markets, leaders and policymakers can craft the future of our cities. I hope I will provide some insight into where we are currently, why it's so important to understand how we got here, why we need to care about where we're going, and, most of all, how we get there.

Acknowledgements

This book has been writing itself in my mind for more years than I care to remember. I am deeply grateful to Diane Coyle for suggesting that I actually write it and to

Richard Baggaley, Sam Clark and Jonathan Wainwright for publishing it. The brunt of the various obsessions written up here – and the frequent absences, physical and mental, to which they have given rise – has been borne by my family and friends. Sorry and thank you.

I am especially grateful for support from my daughter Jess, who has provided invaluable editing and research, and from Angeliki, with whose 2016 spring and summer I took significant liberties. Colleagues past (John Holden) and present (Irene Guillet) have also provided research support. The opportunities to work with a variety of international cities afforded to me by Debra Mountford and colleagues at the OECD LEED Programme have been invaluable. I am grateful for comments from Jess Emmerich, Kevin Fenning, John Holden, Tristram Hunt, John Kingman, Max Nathan, Henry Overman, Brian Robson, Angeliki Stogia, Tony Travers and Michael Ward. The influence on me of the work of the late Asa Briggs and Peter Hall as well as that of Nick Crafts, Eric Evans and Tristram Hunt goes way beyond the extensive references I make to their work. I hope I have done justice to it. But in this and every other regard, the shortcomings of this book are mine alone.

Introduction

British cities are coming back from the brink, finally recovering from the economic and social damage inflicted on them by deindustrialization. Yet even after some of the most purposeful civic leadership ever seen in this country, most of the UK's cities remain economically and politically weak. Labour, Coalition and Conservative governments have for most of the past three decades had explicit commitments to narrow regional differentials, with an increasing focus on cities as the engines of growth, but the UK remains one of the most centralized countries in Europe, with London dominating the economy and politics.

This may be changing. The last Labour government's very tentative experimentation with devolution gave way to more progress through City Deals under the 2010–15 Coalition. George Osborne became their champion during the latter period of the Coalition and after the Conservative election victory of 2015. Theresa May's administration looks like it will carry on the process, seeming to recognize the need to deliver on the challenges of Brexit and the *cri de coeur* from the British people for more responsive and engaged government.

The decision to leave the European Union shook the British political system. It will be years before we know the full economic consequences but its political consequences are already centre stage. For the foreseeable future the fate of the UK government will hinge as much as anything on its ability to make the parts of Britain that were damaged by industrial decline feel some hope. A great many of these areas are urban: cities and their satellite towns. City self-government must be part of the answer to the Brexit challenge.

This book is both personal odyssey and economic history. Urban Britain was in decline for decades. I link the story of absolute decline in our lifetimes to the world into which my parents were born, less than a century ago, when people spoke of Manchester and Glasgow in the same way we talk about Shanghai today: as a global centre of growth. The slump in fortunes of the economies of the great cities of the North, the Midlands and Scotland goes back a long way. Understanding it requires us to revisit the birth of our modern cities: to identify the reasons for their growth and subsequent decline in the following decades.

Britain was the first predominantly urban nation on earth. Now a majority of the world's people live in cities. Having got there ahead of the world by some 150 years, how have we contrived to become a nation whose cities are so weak? This question is the first issue I address in this book. Unless we understand how and why the decline of our cities happened, there is a grave danger that we will continue the charade of so much recent British public life, pretending the whole country is faring well, or that we know the quick fixes for those parts that are not. Chapter 1 explains that Britain's urban industrial development had peculiar early features that created the mould for what followed, characterized by low investment and low levels of skills. These contributed to a poor record of innovation, which in turn made it hard for the centres of the Industrial Revolution to evolve and grow after their early period of vitality.

This is the context for the revival in the economies of British cities in recent years that is also described in chapter 1. The nature of growth has changed and the service-driven economy is finding what it needs in cities. Smaller and more southerly cities have been growing well for years, but there are positive signs in all the big old cities of the Industrial Revolution, and in the mill and mining towns too. However, regional differentials aren't narrowing – they are growing as London continues on its turbocharged path.

We need to look more deeply at cities and at the very nature of urbanization for an explanation. Chapter 2 therefore looks at cities as places: at the DNA of cities and how it expresses itself in their institutions, at governance, at public services, and at the role of religion and culture. Just as the earlier urban economic model depended on strong firms, which turned out in fact to be relatively weak, British cities had underdeveloped governance in terms both of municipal authorities and in the organization of business. Religion played a key role for a time, but its influence faded. When viewed through the lens of culture, we see that the cities failed to create productive cultural capital that would endure once the economic tide turned. As a result, economic change, rather than helping to replenish the stock of companies, jobs, knowledge and culture, sapped their vitality: our cities started slowly, but inexorably, to weaken and decline.

There are signs this is reversing. Chapter 3 documents the journey of political centralization that happened in the UK, and the more recent story of the moves we have seen towards devolution. Just as economic growth looks to have become more urban in recent years, we are seeing strong political pressure for city growth. The chapter concludes with guarded optimism about the future of cities.

The first part of this book draws on the literature on the economic history of the UK and of British cities, painting a picture of their rise and fall. It draws equally on the burgeoning body of research into modern urban performance in economics and geography to gauge what is happening today. It concludes that Britain's cities are once again growing, although they have a long journey ahead.

Much that is written about the future of cities tries (and fails) to draw transferable international lessons for the UK. It is just not possible for a city like Birmingham to import directly the lessons of Barcelona or Copenhagen. Reality constrains the art of the possible; social scientists would point to cities' 'path dependence' and 'institutional thickness': the fact that history and politics have shaped them as they are. But the story of Victorian cities is ours. We should learn from it.

As in the early Victorian age, one city in the UK is perhaps leading the way more than others. Manchester, as well as being the place where I grew up and currently live, happens to be that city, and consequently plays a particularly prominent role in this story. Manchester is not unique and not all of the lessons it offers are positive ones, as we shall see. The experience of other cities – historical, local and international – is also used extensively, all with the same purpose: to inform the agenda set out here for making Britain's cities as strong as they can be.

The book's final chapter sets out this new agenda for British cities, using the opportunity of political decentralization to liberate their economies, their businesses, civic authorities, universities and communities. I argue that we need to focus on getting the economies of the biggest city regions motoring, to start to build momentum.

Above all, the UK needs a devolutionary ratchet, allowing major cities the freedom to seek devolution of any area of public spending that is not inherently national in nature. Cities should have powers to raise some of their own taxes, including business, property and sales-based taxes, and to increase them. They will also need to be subject to due scrutiny from the National Audit Office. If there is real evidence of failure, the national government will have to be able to step in, but only on rare occasions and with a super-majority vote in parliament.

In terms of policies, three areas are pivotal. Sustained investment in transport and infrastructure is one, requiring large sums and devolved decision-making; national decision makers have systematically underinvested outside London and the south of England. So too is an innovation-centric industrial policy, although – after a gap of a generation in daring to think about public sector coordination and intervention – much remains to be understood about how to implement this. Investment in people is essential, and again decisions must be made at a devolved level; Whitehall meddles (and has been cutting funding for further education and adult training) without any knowledge about the skills needed in different parts of the country.

Alongside the book's specific policy proposals is the recurring theme of the need to 'do' policy differently. We need to build and sustain strong markets, but we also need to emphasize the social fabric of cities – their institutions, companies, government and communities are at least as important as policy analysis and funding. This includes making sure work is available to those with no up-to-date skills, through publicly funded temporary community jobs for people who would otherwise be claiming benefits.

Devolving power to cities affords an opportunity to link these areas of policy at a manageable scale; certainly, Whitehall constantly fails to coordinate them nationally. However, experimentation is important in every aspect, and nowhere is this more true than in relation to community, and the organizations – economic, social and cultural – that make each place distinctive. If we do everything else discussed above but neglect the need to support people and the communities in which they live, we will have failed to learn one of the most important lessons from our history.

Chapter 1

The invention and reinvention of the modern city

Understanding the history of our cities

A century ago, economic historians observed that UK exports looked over-dependent on the Manchester-based textiles industry, which was passing its peak. The same vulnerability looks to be even more the case with London-based financial services today. London's financial service success has quite literally paid for a period in which the rest of the country has been wrestling with the later stages of industrial decline, providing many of the jobs in the city centres that have grown over recent years. But our domestic economy is over reliant on this sector and the cast iron certainty with which people assumed London would remain dominant in the world has been corroded by the decision of the British people to leave the European Union. The future of Britain's financial sector looks less certain than it has for decades.

One account of the British economy in the period before World War I reads ominously like something that historians may yet write in respect of financial services today:

> There were some signs even before 1914 that Britain had become excessively dependent on dealings with the outside world and paid too little attention to the use of home resources. Competition from Germany and the United States challenged her old easy supremacy, and she was dilatory in adapting herself to new conditions. More than half her whole exports was textiles, and too large a part of her foreign earnings came from the vulnerable market for cotton textiles, increasingly likely to be threatened by competition from new producers.[2]

With or without Brexit (but all the more so with it), Britain needs to take a long hard look at how, as a nation, we intend to sustain and improve our standard of living and reduce the costs of economic failure, not least in our cities.

There are economic and social costs to the very heavily centralized nature of the British economy. There is also a theoretical model in which some regions of the country produce the tax revenue and others receive the benefit, with the fiscal and monetary union of the UK providing a measure of equalization such that the welfare of everywhere is sustained. That is the model we have tended

towards in the last forty years. The economic centralization of the nation has been compounded by political
centralization, making power feel in every sense remote
from most parts of England.[3] But this model has economic costs, as many parts of the country are far away
from a fully value-maximizing equilibrium. It has social
costs too, in that, over time, the tendency of markets to
exaggerate any dynamic has seen the higher-value productive capacity of the UK become more concentrated in
ever fewer places. Young people, and some older ones,
move south, but communities, unsurprisingly, remain
rooted. The referendum on Britain's membership of the
EU seems to suggest that this model of development has
created divides between the relatively few parts of the
country that feel prosperous and the many that do not.

The referendum result is clearly complex, but one
reading is that a country that feels it has no stake in
southern financial-services-led growth has put at risk
the sector upon which, in very material ways, it most
depends. The result could yet become a tragedy if the
strong signs of economic progress in many cities in the
last decade are put at risk by the outcome of the referendum. Manchester, Liverpool, Bristol and Newcastle
are all cities that voted to remain in the EU. They feel an
optimism borne from growing markets for high-value
services, health and higher education, and from a lively
and improving cultural life too. Some would argue, pejo-
ratively, that these cities have become 'London-lite', and

that they too are part of the problem – that its now time to spread the jobs out further.

It is certainly true that many cities in the UK now have, at their core, a sense of optimism, vibrancy and even prosperity. Perhaps this makes them feel a tiny bit like London. The important question is why so few places in the country feel like this in the first place. The challenge is to change that without a kneejerk response that uses scarce public funds or heavy-handed regulation to try to 'even-out' growth unsustainably. Our economic geography, and indeed some of the logic of Brexit, has been 200 years in the making. It is incredibly important now to understand how we got here, and what made and unmade our cities, so that we can proceed on a sure footing as we seek to grasp their potential for the future.

Cities and the Industrial Revolution

Britain is one of the world's most urban nations, and it was the first. Civilization has always been urban, but until quite recently the world has been predominantly rural. A tenth of Europe's medieval population lived in cities, the sizes of which grew steadily but far from continuously. The clustering forces of economic growth were interrupted by plague and war and were initially limited by the need for fortification, the availability of natural resources and the self-interest of urban dwellers and their guilds.[4] Compared with the great cities of Europe, Britain was backward, being aptly described by a Venetian traveller at the end of the fifteenth century as 'thinly inhabited' with 'scarcely any towns of importance'.[5]

In the middle of the seventeenth century London had a population of less than 400,000 and the largest other British cities, York and Norwich, had barely 30,000 each. The urban population of the UK rose in a period of proto-industrialization in the eighteenth century. By 1800 some 20% of the total population lived in urban areas, at which point London's population was around a million, with Birmingham, Manchester, Liverpool and Bristol in the region of 70,000 and Leeds and Sheffield comfortably less than half that size. It was the 1851 census that found that more than half the UK's resident population lived in towns and cities. This was a first for any country; the world as a whole has reached this point only in the last five years or so. Britain was the first nation to be predominantly both urban and industrialized.[6] By 1880, 80% of the population was urban, with the proportion working in manufacturing a little under two-thirds (up from two-fifths eighty years earlier). Conversely, between 1800 and 1871 the proportion of the workforce working in agriculture and fisheries declined from 35% to just 15%.[7] In this respect Britain's performance was revolutionary, moving labour from agriculture to industry on a very large scale in the early industrial period.[8]

The population of cities exploded in a process that was both driving economic change and being driven by it. But a major cultural change was also taking place. Much manufacturing had been done at home in the country, outside regulated town guilds, in earlier periods. Towns and even cities were principally administrative and religious centres, commercial hubs and markets. The Industrial Revolution was to change not just the size of our urban areas, but also their locations and functions, creating a new urban system with much of the growth in urban areas unconstrained by traditional patterns of development and the societal norms with which they were associated.

Why was Britain the first country to industrialize? There are several explanations (and a vast literature).[9] High pre-existing levels of wealth and income played a part. So did an early and wholehearted engagement with the Enlightenment and its notion of 'useful knowledge' that would power innovation. A strong economy, relatively strong civil society and institutions, and a mercantile orientation all played a role too, as did a capitalist revolution in agriculture.[10] But why cities?

Which cities grew and why?

There is no single explanation as to why cities and industrialization happened first – and happened when they did – in Britain. Chance was a part of the story, as

British inventors stumbled across innovations, but the prior evolution of the British economy was much more important and five factors seem to have played a key role: geography, raw materials, people, our use of capital, and technology.[11]

Geography and climate

Northern England's mild, damp climate was well suited to spinning and weaving (and the wool its sheep produced had meant a head start in textiles know-how). More importantly, the ready supply of water from the Pennines provided the early source of power for the mills. Relative population density was important too, in providing markets. And as a small island, nowhere is too far from a navigable river and a port in Britain, and transport was relatively well developed.

Raw materials

More than any other single raw material, it was cotton that drove the growth of industrial Britain: it was spun and weaved in ever-increasing quantities, with the cotton emanating largely from America rather than the British colonies in the Indian subcontinent. The new machines and the factory system to which they gave rise transformed cotton production. Together, the towns and cities that produced textiles were the game changers in the early industrial age, creating an industry that, by the early 1840s, accounted for more than 70% of the total value of exports[12] and created the mould for British industry. The new industry created a demand both for coal to power steam engines and for an engineering industry to make the new and ever-more-sophisticated cotton machinery that was needed, as well as the steam engines and other tools of the trade. Britain's reserves of coal and their proximity to major urban centres were a factor here too, providing cheap energy – another distinguishing feature of Britain's economy in the period.[13]

Labour

The Industrial Revolution needed people, lots of them, and they weren't to be found in the towns and cities of the time. Changes in agriculture, the Enclosure Acts and developments in agricultural technology rendered surplus to requirements thousands of smallholders, yeoman farmers and even larger numbers of landless labourers. They looked to the emerging cities for work. The Irish Potato Famine of the mid 1840s led to large-scale migration too, with 40,000 Irish arriving in Manchester and Glasgow and 100,000 in London. By 1851 the Irish made up 5.6% of London's population, 13% of Manchester's and 18% of Glasgow's. Irish migration was to continue, and they were followed later by a significant number of Germans and other Europeans. The result of

this was growth of quite staggering proportions. Sheffield's population more than doubled in the forty years
to 1841, while Leeds tripled in size to over 150,000, and
Manchester grew from 95,000 to 310,000. At the start of
the period of industrialization labour was expensive – a
major factor in spurring innovation and driving demand
for the products of industrialization[14] thereafter – real
wages fell but population growth continued.

Capital

Early Industrial Britain was a freewheeling world. It had
its dotcom-style booms and busts in which some investments failed, such as canals of dubious value that could
bankrupt their funders. The emphasis here is on the kind
of capital that was available and the ability to access it.
The evidence tends to suggest that the volume of capital was not a driver of change in comparison to other
economies.[15] Some of the earliest investment went into
transport: canals and turnpike roads aimed at moving
agricultural produce and coal. The landed gentry funded
much of this. So the aristocracy played a big role both
in proto-industrialization and, by dramatically improving
agricultural output, in creating the conditions for a sustainable population increase. But most factories were
small and were funded through capital raised through
informal means, such as from money-lenders, local
banks and money markets. This meant that 'men from

relatively humble backgrounds could establish businesses and rely on a combination of commercial skill and
good fortune for success'.[16]

Technology

Technological development – the invention of new
machines and techniques and their widespread application – played a major role. The spinning jenny (invented
in 1764) and later Richard Arkwright's water frame (1769)
and Samuel Crompton's mule (1779) were to change
textile production, as was James Watt's steam engine
(1765). Society and culture in Britain were amenable to
the spread of ideas and tinkering with new inventions.

The earliest factories were in rural Derbyshire and
elsewhere in the East Midlands. Arkwright's water
frame, powered by water near Derby, was where it all
began. But the North West became the heartland of
industrialization through Arkwright's subsequent development in Lancashire, the early adoption of the steam
engine in Manchester, and then Crompton's mule. More
important than any one invention (including steam) was
what recent economic historians such as Joel Mokyr and
Nick Crafts term micro-innovations or gadgets.[17] So while
there were great leaps in technology, there was incre-
mental and small-scale innovation too. These, rather
than steam power, were what seem to have driven the
early part of the Industrial Revolution.

There are two particularly striking features of British urban industrial growth.

The first was that Britain, particularly in the cotton towns, had a series of endowments, advantages and good fortune that made what happened here happen first, and more intensively, than elsewhere in the world. Part of the reason for this was that many investors, and particularly wealthy landowners (uncharacteristically by European standards), invested freely and entrepreneurially, caring little for the customs and tastes of the time.[18]

The second was that the things that made British urban life bloom in the late eighteenth century are remarkably similar to the factors that determine success in modern urban ecosystems. This is a point picked up by Peter Hall in his monumental work *Cities in Civilisation*.[19] It is particularly so in what it tells us about why the towns around Manchester became a case study for industrialization. Recent econometric analysis confirms that most of the economy was characterized by unspectacular growth and limited innovation in the early nineteenth century. It was the towns and cities of the cotton industry, along with the iron industry, that were revolutionary.[20]

Manchester's early industrialization had given the city and its hinterland a series of endowments to service the needs of entrepreneurs. The city was unencumbered by the restrictive guild traditions of 'older cities' (the Weavers Act of 1588 freed the textiles industry from medieval regulations), a factor in making the place freer for migrants to settle and thrive.[21] It was better networked too, which was perhaps linked to the fact that a large proportion of the city's inhabitants were religious dissenters in one of the few places where they felt at home. Manchester established learned institutions early, which hot-housed new innovations. These factors combined in what Peter Hall describes as

> the world's first innovative milieu: an environment which gave rise to a constant, synergistic ferment of technical and organisational improvement in products and processes.[22]

Nick Crafts goes further, arguing that cotton was the exceptional industry, associated with the clustering of the industry in Lancashire, driven by the agglomeration effects of a micro-innovatory hothouse.[23] The rest of the textiles industry in the North and the growth of shipbuilding in Glasgow, on the Tyne and elsewhere were fundamental drivers of the economy in the nineteenth century, but they tended to be evolutionary, not revolutionary, in their operation and from the point of view of the aggregate performance of the UK economy.[24]

What went wrong?

Britain's cities went from being the workshops of the world to, until quite recently, being seen by many as lost causes.[25] We will see later how many urban areas are recovering well, such that the word renaissance might reasonably be used to describe what is afoot. But between the 1870s (or a little later) and the 1990s, urban Britain went first into relative decline and then into steady and then rapid absolute decline. What went wrong, when and why?

Let us start with the question of when decline happened, which is possibly the most contested question of all. It is popularly thought that the decline of cities is a post-war phenomenon. It is particularly associated with the end of the long boom in the 1970s, as OPEC flexed its muscles, jacking up oil prices in 1973 and again in 1980, just as Britain's industrial relations climate was approaching its nadir. But to take one example, cotton production peaked during World War I, even though it was decades later that the substantial absolute decline materialized. So the roots of urban decline may be very deep, even if it was during the period after World War II that the physical signs of decline started to emerge.

An over-concern with physical development?

Our post-war concern with the physical rebuilding of cities has coloured our view of when decline started, perhaps excessively so. War damage took a long time to repair and there was a significant legacy of poorly built and maintained Victorian housing to be tackled. Much money was invested in rebuilding. But there is an argument that post-war modernism was as destructive as the Luftwaffe in wrecking the urban form of British cities, creating often shoddily built housing and dysfunctional urban environments.[26] As Jane Jacobs reminds us in the context of the US, 'slumming and unslumming' often happen in ways that run counter to the ideas of city planners, however grand the design or large the regeneration budget.[27] All of these factors are part of the story. But if, as this brief overview suggests, there are signs that the economies of urban areas were faltering before then, in the early years of the twentieth century and before, it is there that we need to look for the origin of the problem. After all, the physical environment is far from being the most important factor in driving city growth. As Peter Hall points out, the populations of many of the most successful cities in history have sought to escape rural poverty by moving into highly insanitary, badly built and badly designed environments, sometimes to the detriment of their own health. They have done so and continue to do so around the world for economic betterment (though more urban societies also seem happier than rural ones[28]) for themselves and their families. So it is to the motor of the urbanization process – the economy – that we need to look for the origins of decline.

The origins of decline?

Did British cities decline for some innate reasons or was it because of general industrial and economic decline across the country? Causality probably runs both ways. There is relatively little research specifically on the economy of urban Britain in the late Victorian period, but there is extensive analysis on the performance of the British economy as a whole. Given that it was urban Britain that led industrialization, looking at what happened to the British economy in the late nineteenth century and leading up to World War I probably gives us a pretty good picture.

Population growth, which had created the capacity for industrial growth in cities, continued pretty much unabated through the nineteenth century. Indeed, it accelerated in some cities (Newcastle in particular) towards the end of the century. Even Greater Manchester, which had grown so much in the early part of the period, added an additional million people in the period from 1861 to 1901, falling only in 1941, a decade after the UK population had dipped.[29] The late nineteenth century saw the start of large-scale emigration from the UK to the US, Australia and elsewhere. This may have contributed to something of a brain drain but numerically made little difference to the overall demographic picture of the UK.

So if it wasn't falling population that drove decline, was it falling capital investment? Here, too, the data suggest otherwise. Capital investment was high and rising in mid-Victorian England. For example, between 1865 and 1875 capital investment rose by 40% in value, or perhaps by even more according to some estimates.[30] Indeed, Alex Cairncross believed that the early 1870s saw a higher proportion of national income saved and invested than perhaps had ever previously been the case. One feature of this period was large-scale international investment. This was, after all, the age of high empire, but housing and railways were also major beneficiaries, as was industry. Staple industries were innovating: the introduction of the ring traveller, for example, saw the efficiency of the cotton industry rise very rapidly from the 1860s onwards. The woollen industry increasingly adopted the more modern technology of the cotton industry. But it was in engineering – both heavy engineering and in machine tools – that new innovation and high investment started to drive major industrial change.

Competition was strong in this period too. Summing up the mid to late Victorian period, one historian concludes that much was working well in the British economy at this time:

> There was probably no period when more genuine competition prevailed, when established interests put few obstacles in the path of the newcomer. The concentration of population in towns and the emergence of a generation that had known none but an industrial way of life provided a larger, more conveniently located pool of workers adapted to the

needs of the time; and educational facilities were just about sufficient to ensure a supply of skill adequate to maintain the momentum of the economy, though there was no margin to spare. Those activities (fundamental to every other branch of the economy) which needed capital in large quantities could obtain it more easily than before.[31]

Unsurprisingly, then, industrial production increased markedly in the late nineteenth century: the output of British industry doubled between 1870 and 1913.

Yet something was changing at this time. During the same period in which British industrial output doubled, world economic output saw a fourfold increase. As a result, Britain went from producing one-third of all output to just one-seventh. The economic origins of decline lie in the erosion of British dominance in staple industries, centred in the major cities. International competition was intensifying. First-mover advantage was diminishing.

It is worth looking at some of the key factors again: education and skills, investment and innovation. These issues do seem to be important in the story of decline because of the character of the British economy.

Child labour and the education of children

Education played a limited role in the lives of most working people in the pre- and early-industrial period, with exposure to education being as much as anything a function of industrial regulation, with the steady reduction in the involvement of children in the workplace increasing the scope for formal education. Education was not considered to be a state function in cities until late in the nineteenth century. Much more than in relation to health (considered later), the burden of education fell on the Church, with the Sunday school movement providing the bulk of schooling. Estimates vary on school enrolment, but many fewer than 2 million children were in education in the late 1830s, and even then this was a rudimentary affair with the children of the newly industrializing areas less likely than their rural and small-town counterparts to receive formal schooling.

But what of later development? Economists such as Sascha Becker argue that later technological development required higher levels of education. There is evidence both that Protestant countries were better at providing it and that some of the second wave of industrializers, notably Prussia, placed a higher emphasis on education and secured higher returns.[32] The international data would appear to support the first of these points. Comparative international analysis shows that the UK was a laggard in education, particularly in the 1830s and 1840s, when we had first-mover advantage.[33] In 1830 school enrolment rates in England were 27%, compared with 39% in France, 55% in the US and 69% in Germany. Other countries used education to catch up, which set them up well for what followed:

For it is at this juncture [the turn of twentieth century] that a cluster of innovations, sometimes called the 'second industrial revolution', based on a much greater use of applied science and research came to exert a strong influence on productivity growth and raised the rate of return to investment in human capital.[34]

Levels of education did therefore become much more important during the later stages of industrialization. This meant that the higher levels observed in key competitor countries probably gave them an advantage that was even greater than that conferred by subsequent catch-up in English levels. Criticisms that the country was not investing enough in education and skills also echo through the period.

Technical skills

Of course formal education is only part of the human capital equation. In many respects it is the foundation upon which technical education is based. Writing in 1887, the chairman of the Royal Commission on the State of Technical Education was in no doubt that the formal school system was, by then, a barrier to British progress:

In the first place, technical education, although a most important branch, is only one branch of national education.

If national education is bad, technical education cannot be good. Neither the workman, nor the foreman, nor the designer, nor the employer can profit by a technical training unless he has first been trained to use his mind and to feel pleasure in using it... The first step, therefore, in establishing a complete system of technical education is to supply as far as possible all deficiencies in our system of general education; and more especially to perfect our elementary and intermediate schools.[35]

While the Commission was of the view that British workshops provided better artisan skills, its chairman also noted that competitor nations were catching up, describing at length the role played by the Swiss and German Polytechnics:

The number of the Polytechnic Schools of Germany is much in excess of the actual demand for technical instruction. In the early part of this century the Germans found themselves immeasurably inferior in practical knowledge to countries like England. They were obliged to learn in the schools, if anywhere, much that Englishmen could learn in the workshop. Again, a generous emulation moved the States of Germany to vie with one another in making liberal provision for every branch of learning. [36]

So even a generation before British industry hit its peak production in key industries and relative decline turned into absolute decline, it was known that the level of formal education was inadequate. It was known, too, that British technical skills relied more heavily on provision in the workplace than was the case in our newly emerging competitors. Britain was also aware that competitor nations were designing and investing – maybe even overinvesting – in centres of learning: something we sought to emulate without ever, in many respects, succeeding. As Nick Crafts states:

> Although educational spending as a fraction of GDP rose, it fell further behind the United States and Germany such that in 1900, while Britain spent 1.3 per cent of GDP on education, the US spent 1.7 per cent and Germany 1.9 per cent. At the turn of the century, when it seems probable that returns to investment in human capital were rising, the rate of accumulation of skills per worker estimated by Williamson rose in the United States to 0.57 per cent a year compared with 0.30 per cent in Britain.[37]

The best conclusion to be drawn is that Britain was underinvesting in skills and seemed very poor at putting scientists and their knowledge to use in businesses. The training and investment in human capital we did have was heavily dependent on a relatively weakening industrial base of companies. Perhaps most importantly, Britain looks to have underinvested in a robust system of institutions to compensate for this compared with our international competitors. It wasn't just companies and governments that were to blame. So too organizations like the Institution of Mechanical Engineers, which in the period leading up to World War I refused to recognize technical education as an important part of an engineer's training.[38]

Capital

Did the British economy have a capital problem in this later period of industrialization? The answer to this question turns on a view as to whether or not the relatively internationally oriented nature of the British economy served in some way to distort capital investment either in terms of volume or priorities at home. William Ashworth:

> The situation may be summarised as one in which the British economy at the beginning of the twentieth century passed from its remarkable late Victorian growth to a condition, by no means stagnant or declining, but showing slower progress. And the main reasons for the change were a failure to exploit favourable economic conditions at home and even greater concentration than before on dealings with the outside world in circumstances in which the advantages from so doing could not go on increasing so easily as they had done a little earlier.[39]

There are two key questions that arise from this. First, did the international orientation of the UK economy mean that there was less focus on the domestic market despite favourable economic conditions? (Could investment in British firms have enabled more exports rather than investment stoking up foreign competition?) Second, was there a failure to exploit potential domestic markets? The evidence tends to suggest that the first was not the issue.[40] Causality may in fact have worked the other way around. Britain never had a particularly capital-intensive mode of development and had become locked into that by this period, with capital seeking new international markets to secure a return. On the second question, there is evidence both of inefficiency and poor capital market discipline on management and of information imperfections.[41]

Ashworth places the decline of formerly vigorous urban markets at the heart of the changes that were underway:

> As time went on, however, a diminishing proportion of people had their business prospects dominated by the state of a localised market and local banking arrangements. The creation of a national and then an international system of rapid transport and communication, matched by the establishment of similarly comprehensive financial arrangements, broke down many remnants of local self-containment and directly exposed most economic activities to the unifying influence of national or global market conditions.[42]

The UK economy went through cycles with major upswings, notably in the years before the outbreak of World War II. Peak coal production occurred in 1912, with cotton following a year or two later, but the global economy was still generally growing. The industries of the towns and cities that had fuelled industrialization were most likely sweating outdated machinery with a relatively low-skilled workforce, declining in market power even as the British economy relied on them for its export earnings. More importantly from an economic point of view, as we have seen, this is likely to have happened in part because of the particular kind of development Britain had gone through. The UK had relatively low levels of investment in human and financial capital, an overreliance on firm-based rather than institutionally supported arrangements for skill supply, and an international orientation focused on relatively low-value-added sectors.

Britain industrialized and urbanized via a model of (relatively) high wages, access to markets and the availability of cheap energy. These were less important drivers in the late nineteenth century than they had been earlier. To the extent they still mattered, the evidence suggests that the US rather than the British economy had the advantage by this point.[43] There was a window in which the urban economies of Britain could have adapted from a position of strength. They failed to do so.

The geography of decline and growth

The Barlow Commission on the Distribution of the Industrial Population, which reported in 1940, summarized the country's changing economic geography well. It noted that the distribution of the population reflects that of industry, and that the growing industries of the pre-World War II period were more footloose in the sense of not requiring proximity to raw materials. It also

noted that the era of cheap power and improving transport had rendered these factors less important anyway,
and that they were, even then, tending to locate near
markets, in London and the Home Counties. Moreover, it
concluded, there was no reason to think that this trend
would end.[44]

One of the fundamental lessons from Peter Hall's work
is that history tells us that cities rise and fall. Geopolitical
shifts and/or technological or other essentially economic
phenomena did in Britain what they do everywhere. The
precise mixture of these that precipitated decline in Britain continues to be contested by historians, but some
observations can still be made. First, as tempting as it is
to blame empire and the internationalization of British
commercial interests, the data, described above, suggest that the blame should be laid elsewhere. The British
share of growing international markets fell even when
the conditions at home were propitious. So, despite its
many inherited advantages, relatively at first, and absolutely as the twentieth century wore on, the UK started
to slow and, in many industries, to fall behind.

A failure to innovate is almost certainly a part of the
story. Peter Hall again:

> One thing only is certain: as the examples of Manchester and
> Glasgow show, cities that falter in the innovative process
> soon stumble, and their industrial base dies. Leaders in one
> generation will soon be harried by new competitors, coming
> up from behind; and unless they either develop new ways of

producing old specialities, or better still derive entirely new products out of old traditions, they will be overtaken and disappear into industrial oblivion.[45]

Asa Briggs describes the heyday of British cities as the era between the coming of the railway and the arrival of the motorcar. Both of these developments were general-purpose technologies (GPTs), allowing every industry they affected to create more output with a given set of inputs, creating wealth to spur subsequent rounds of growth.[46] The Industrial Revolution that started with cotton spinning and ended with railways delineates the first of these. But after a few decades the advantage of this first wave of GPTs – which British cities had been at the leading edge of – gave way to a second round (such as electricity and the internal combustion engine), in the early part of the twentieth century, in which the UK economy played a major but less absolutely central role. More recently, a third wave of such technologies has been the revolution in information and communications technology and the advent of modern computing. Even if some economists such as Robert Gordon argue that it isn't as significant as earlier waves,[47] possibly with less job-creating potential as a result, British towns and cities have played a more modest role, though scientifically a very important one.

To illustrate, look at the three waves of GPTs through the lens of Manchester. The city was at the centre of the first Industrial Revolution, had the first Ford car plant outside the US during the second wave (as well as being where Rolls met Royce), and, after the war, saw Alan Turing's work fulfilled in the creation of the world's first fully programmable computer: a key staging post in the creation of the third wave. The key point is this. Only in the first of these three waves did Manchester internalize the benefit of the scientific and technological breakthroughs, creating very large numbers of businesses and jobs over a sustained period of time. Something went wrong in Manchester, which at least played a role in all three waves of technological innovation. Other nineteenth-century towns and cities remained even more firmly grounded in their original industrial base. The result was that a great many of these saw their economies undermined both by the weakening of the UK's competitive position in staple industries and by a failure to adapt. Indeed, it is argued that those urban areas that have been most successful in the innovation economy in recent decades are precisely not the great Victorian centres but smaller places, often (though not always) with a strong university, a more southern location and a quite different set of attributes to the great nineteenth-century cities.[48] And of course, unlike the era of the railways that favoured point-to-point traffic between relatively dense populations, the era of the motorcar enabled the creation of a more dispersed – one might say American – mode of development. British density, once a strength, seemed less so in the twentieth century. Asa Briggs talked of the railways banishing feudalism in the nineteenth century. The age of the motorcar has been one of an even deeper individual freedom. These are economic facts but also cultural realities too. Perhaps it is to the culture of the British economy that we need to look for further explanation.

Economists, frustrated by the limited explanatory power of the data, are looking to the other, sociological factors that lie behind the British model of growth. It is to a broadly defined notion of social capital that the Bank of England's Andy Haldane reached in looking at the conundrums of modern Britain.[49]

Building on Hall's notion of an 'innovative milieu', what we might perhaps conclude is that Manchester and other urban areas had characteristics that, in the long run, may not have served them well. The entrepreneurs of the early nineteenth century were practical people who paid only what they needed to, trained only as much as was necessary, and paid less heed to formal and technical education institutions than did Britain's competitors. This became the pattern, and locked much of urban Britain into that path. The earliest industrialists weren't to know it but their ecosystem may have been less adaptable and less attractive to investment in the long run than those created by later entrants. Their choices may even have played a role in limiting the lifespan of the golden age of British cities.

It is worth pausing to reflect on just how risky it is for an economy to be heavily dependent on so few industries, and how widespread and deep the decline in British cities was when that economic dependence unravelled.

Decline and recovery

The rapid growth of the UK population seen throughout the nineteenth century and in the early twentieth gave way to more modest and halting progress in the post-war period, until the 1990s when migration to the UK increased the rate of growth again. But within the total, the population of cities generally fell through the post-war period, until the 1990s. Some of these falls were dramatic, with Liverpool, for example, seeing its population fall from a peak of 870,000 in the mid 1930s to 430,000 in 2001. Recovery has only come recently. All the major conurbations apart from London lost population during the period of the most intense economic restructuring, from 1981 to 1991, and even London managed only a 0.4% increase. Many of these conurbations saw falls in population in the subsequent decade too, with only London among the major cities growing at all in this period. So the UK had an urban population but it was not urbanizing in any consistent way. Only in the period from 2001 is there a more consistent urbanizing trend, and even then the pattern is far from uniform.[50]

The unevenness is striking. Looking at table 1 overleaf, while the large conurbations largely fared badly up to 2001, some smaller towns and cities did rather well. Since then, the major conurbations have started to see growth for the first time in decades. The reason for this lies not in the demographics but, rather, in the economics.

What is driving growth now?

Two linked phenomena have driven urban growth in the UK over recent years. First, structural change, the technological basis and trading impact of which have shifted the British economy (and others) towards a more urban form of development. Second, as the growing sectors of production have become more urban, these places have become more important centres of consumption too.[51] So, although the UK remains highly urbanized, some cities have grown, others have declined and some of the latter have 'resurged', at least in terms of population change.

The first and most important of these phenomena is continuing deindustrialization. This process is particularly marked in cities where the concentration of traditional industry was highest to start with. Merseyside is perhaps the most obvious example in table 1 (overleaf), though other places look quite similar. Second, the growth of service industries is marked in some areas,

Table 1. Urban population 1981–2011.

	Change 1981–1991 (%)	Change 1991–2001 (%)	Change 2001–2011 (%)
Conurbations			
London	0.4	7.0	14.0
Tyne and Wear	−2.8	−4.3	2.7
Merseyside	−5.5	−5.0	1.4
Greater Manchester	−2.5	−1.6	8.1
West Midlands	−2.0	−1.9	7.1
West Yorkshire	−0.2	1.1	7.1
South Yorkshire	−2.2	−1.7	6.1
Large non-metropolitan cities			
Cardiff	3.5	3.5	13.3
Derby UA	2.6	0.1	12.2
Nottingham UA	0.4	−3.7	14.5
Swansea	0.2	−2.7	7.0
Leicester UA	−0.6	0.6	17.8
Aberdeen	0.8	−1.0	5.0
Plymouth UA	−0.8	−4.1	6.5
Stoke-on-Trent UA	−1.2	−3.6	3.5
Edinburgh	−2.2	2.9	6.2
Bristol, City of UA	−2.2	−2.2	12.5
Portsmouth UA	−2.4	0.7	9.8
Southampton UA	−2.4	7.3	8.9
Kingston upon Hull, City of UA	−3.8	−7.6	5.3
Dundee	−8.3	−6.5	1.1

Table 1. *Continued.*

	Change 1981–1991 (%)	Change 1991–2001 (%)	Change 2001–2011 (%)
Small cities			
Lincoln	9.8	1.9	9.3
Worcester	8.0	12.1	5.8
Cambridge	5.7	3.2	13.8
York UA	4.2	5.2	9.4
Exeter	4.2	6.1	7.0
Cheltenham	4.1	2.8	5.2
Gloucester	3.2	6.2	10.7
Preston	2.8	0.4	8.2
Newport	2.3	1.6	6.4
Brighton and Hove UA	1.4	4.0	10.3
Bath and North East Somerset UA	1.0	3.7	4.1
Stirling	0.7	6.6	4.7
Norwich	−0.9	−2.0	9.0
Oxford	−1.1	5.3	13.2
Reading UA	−1.9	7.5	8.8
Durham	−2.1	2.1	—
Middlesbrough UA	−3.9	−6.4	2.6

Source: Adapted from Lupton and Power[52]
and ONS Census 2011.

and has tended to be led by smaller cities and towns (or at least that is where it started). Third, where there has been net growth in manufacturing, this has been led by places other than those where traditional industry was located, as table 2 shows.

Table 2. Deindustrialization and employment change 1960–78.

	As percentage of 1960 employment
London	−42.5
Conurbations	−26.5
Free-Standing Cities	−13.8
Large Towns	−2.2
Small Towns	15.7
Rural Areas	38.0
Great Britain	−11.5

Source: Foresight, Government Office for Science Working Paper (http://bit.ly/2hhEkgg).

In other words, it is nothing like as simple as saying that the traditional cities of the Midlands and the North have lost manufacturing jobs and gained (fewer) service jobs (though this is true). These cities have also failed to deliver a net gain in manufacturing jobs, whereas other places have. Echoing what the Barlow Report foresaw seventy years earlier, Ron Martin *et al.* argue that:

Since the late-1970s, and in common with other Western nations, the UK has been undergoing a fundamental transition to a 'post-industrial', information-based, service economy... The UK's cities ... have lost their traditional role ... and their prosperity now and into the future will depend on finding a new role in this latest phase in the evolution of capitalism.[53]

But this is not just a 1980s issue. It goes back a very long way. Table 3, from the Centre for Cities, illustrates the issue rather well.

Table 3. Growth in jobs 1911–2013.

	City	All jobs growth 1911–2013 (%)		City	All jobs growth 1911–2013 (%)
1	Crawley	598	48	Hull	−2
2	Peterborough	373	49	Birkenhead	−4
3	Oxford	323	50	Liverpool	−10
4	Cambridge	295	51	Huddersfield	−13
5	Swindon	293	52	Bradford	−16
6	Reading	273	53	Bolton	−20
7	Worthing	257	54	Wigan	−25
8	Luton	217	55	Rochdale	−30
9	Bournemouth	204	56	Blackburn	−44
10	Coventry	197	57	Burnley	−51

Source: Centre for Cities report (http://bit.ly/2hhzeR8).[54]

The places that have grown the most jobs over the century to 2013 are smaller cities, places in the commutable London fringe and newer manufacturing towns, with the top ten adding some 750,000 new jobs between them.

Economic decline was concentrated in the bigger local economies. Those cities which in 1911 had more than 100,000 jobs added only 1.1 million, or 22%, in the period to 2013. Those that in 1911 had fewer than 100,000 jobs added another 2.4 million jobs: an increase of 145%.[54]

The early industrializers seem to have been less attractive to newer investment and industry. As the title of a report by James Simmie *et al.* suggests, 'History matters'.[55] They go further, arguing that the history of places determines the limits of the possible, with the capacity of places shaped by historic combinations of knowledge, assets and innovation. Change is difficult. Most industrial cities in the world remain just that.[56] Many cities, including many of the most successful, have proved themselves unwilling or unable to adapt sufficiently to become magnets for newly arriving investment, and are even insufficiently magnetic to retain the functions and people that originated there once their original *raison d'être* has passed.

The reurbanization and recentralization of Britain

In some ways the UK has come full circle. In the pre-industrial era London was dominant, the southern part of the country was prosperous, and the most populous places outside the capital were to be found in the South West and in the east. While this may not be the case in population terms today, it is uncomfortably true in economic terms.

In 2014 (the last year for which data are available), London and the South East accounted for 38% of UK gross value added (GVA) with some 26% of the population. Greater London's GVA per head was 173% of the UK average, up from 160% in 1997, with the South East at 110% in both years. Many parts of the country – including the East and West Midlands, Yorkshire and the Humber – have consequently seen their relative output per head fall relatively over the period. No region outside the south and east of the country has GVA per head significantly above 85% of the UK average. Regional disparities are generally rising, and have done so more over the period since the crash in 2008, with every region in England outside London and the south seeing a fall in GVA per head relative to the national average. But at least the cities, including the bigger and more industrial ones, are generally growing again, and not just in population terms. Table 4 (overleaf) shows that GVA grew in all the big cities (with the exception of Merseyside) during and after the 2008 crash, even if it is still London leading the way with nearly double the rate of growth of Birmingham or Manchester; differentials are widening, not narrowing, at city level too.

Table 4. Five-year GVA growth 2009–14.

Region	Five-year growth (%)
Liverpool	−0.8
Edinburgh	8.4
Bradford	9.2
Leeds	10.5
Cardiff	11.3
Sheffield	12.2
Glasgow	12.9
Belfast	14.1
Greater Manchester	15.2
Birmingham	16.3
Newcastle	18.2
Bristol	19.2
London	28.9

Source: Office for National Statistics (http://bit.ly/2hhC0FS).

Tax and centralization

The industrial age – broadly speaking from the dawn of the nineteenth century to World War I – saw the rise of the great conurbations of the North and the Midlands, and in lowland Scotland too, with these great cities surrounded by smaller towns all of which formed part of an industrial system. Over the course of the twentieth century as industrially centred economies weakened and declined, the centre of gravity of the British economy once more moved south. London proved itself to be more able than other cities to respond to profound decline in manufacturing employment, growing new, high-value-added service industries instead. Moreover, a policy of dispersal of activities from London and, latterly, the constraints on London as it has grown have had an impact on surrounding areas. This is particularly the case with the M4 corridor, which has grown to become the heart of the British economy in recent decades.

Some economists argue that this is simply a factual account of what has happened: the result of market forces we simply have to respect. This might be plausible in a world of perfect labour and capital mobility, but when this is not the case, in the real world, it poses some important challenges. Britain is now among the most economically centralized countries in Europe.[57,58] London and the South East now produce a wildly disproportionate share of the country's tax revenue.

Table 5 (overleaf) shows that with around 14% of the British population London generates 29% of the tax take: nearly nine times more than the country's second biggest city, Manchester, which is a little less than a third the size by population. And London's dominance is growing, providing a quarter more of the tax take in just the decade between 2004 and 2014.[59]

Table 5. Tax take and public spending in selected cities 2004–14.

Rank	City	Share of overall national tax intake 2004/5	Share of overall national tax intake 2014/15	Change in tax generated 2004/5– 2014/15	Change in tax generated between 2004/5 and 2014/15
1	London	25.3%	28.6%	+£28bn	25%
2	Manchester	3.6%	3.3%	+£240m	1%
3	Birmingham	3.3%	3.0%	−£251m	−2%
4	Glasgow	1.9%	1.7%	−£139m	−2%
5	Leeds	1.4%	1.2%	−£151m	−2%

Source: '10 Years of Tax', Centre for Cities.[59]

Research by New Economy in Manchester, working with the Local Government Association, set out the scale of the issue in different terms, estimating the gap between the tax revenues collected in the major conurbations and the amount of money needed to pay for public services (see table 6).

Only the Nottingham area and the city region around Bristol are in surplus. The collective gap, i.e. the deficit between what cities earn and what they spend every year, amounts to £53.5 billion. This is paid for by fiscal transfers and national benefits, the presence of which has prevented US-style collapse in many British cities.[60] Present attempts in England to remove these transfers and their disincentive effect on cities' growth policies need to balance zeal with caution. Bankrupt cities are not an ideal staging post in a renaissance.

Table 6. Public spending and tax take in British conurbations 2013/14.

City Region	Total estimated public expenditure	Total estimated tax take	Gap between spend and tax
Cardiff City Region	£16.3bn	£9.8bn	−£6.5bn
Glasgow and Clyde Valley City Region	£21.4bn	£14.2bn	−£7.2bn
Greater Manchester CA	£27.9bn	£19.8bn	−£8.2bn
Liverpool City Region CA	£17.0bn	£9.5bn	−£7.5bn
North East CA	£20.7bn	£12.5bn	−£8.2bn
Nottingham and Nottinghamshire PCA	£10.5bn	£12.6bn	£2.0bn
Sheffield City Region CA	£13.8bn	£8.8bn	−£5.0bn
West Midlands PCA	£27.4bn	£19.7bn	−£7.7bn
West of England LEP	£10.0bn	£11.6bn	£1.6bn
Leeds city region (estimate)	£26.6bn	£19.6bn	−£7.0bn
Revised core cities total	£191.6bn	£138.0bn	−£53.5bn

Source: New Economy, analysis of UK core cities tax and spend data, 2016.

Theory and Britain's economic geography[61]

When considering the role of cities in national economic growth there are two dominant theoretical perspectives.

The first, associated with geographers and regional economists, focuses on economic efficiency. Persistent regional disparities are argued to be inefficient at the national scale, as they reflect the underutilization of labour and capital in less advanced regions. Regional disparities, it is argued, can also restrict the effectiveness of national macroeconomic measures to support growth, with policies resulting in inflation hotspots and employment bottlenecks. Advocates of this position tend to argue for policy aimed primarily at spatially rebalancing growth.[62]

The second perspective, associated with economists and the 'new economic geography', argues that regional imbalances and spatial agglomeration of economic activity may be efficient and thus positive for national growth. As economic activity naturally gravitates towards certain agglomerations – because of their advantages in terms of business density, access to markets, skilled talent pool, universities, infrastructure and so on – policies that favour the regions that go against these natural agglomeration forces in an attempt to reduce economic disparities may be economically inefficient at the national scale.[63]

Whatever the merits of these perspectives, the geographers' concern for distribution tends to come at the expense of a less convincing account of growth and how and where it can best be stimulated. Conversely, the economists have too little to say about the profound social consequences of their analysis, or the sustainability (or plausibility) of the implied growth model. Taken literally, neither helps those of us whose concern is the exercise of policy choices. Economically, socially and politically, both the creation and the distribution of wealth matter. The key debate is not, therefore, 'growth or distribution' but the trade-offs that policy makers face.

It seems unarguable from the foregoing, and from more recent data too, that a range of factors seem to have shifted development patterns across the world. The era of car-driven sprawl looks to be less dominant. As was discussed earlier, the sectors that are growing seem to favour proximity and density, as do talented young people. As happened 200 years ago in Britain, though for very different reasons (natural endowments are less important than human, scientific and cultural capital, as well as global connectivity), more liberal capital markets and migration have seen agglomeration starting to drive city growth around the world. The problem is that the ability of many British cities, or at least large parts of them, to play a meaningful role in this process seems limited, for the reasons above. These issues are taken up again in chapter 4, which looks at how urban Britain can respond, seeking to drive growth more broadly across the country – all the more important in the light of the Brexit vote. The key point here is that while this kind of growth may be uneven – something that has very undesirable consequences for those left behind – it is possibly the strongest motor of the British economy at the moment. The problem? Left to its own devices, it risks further unbalancing the British economy.

London exceptionalism

There is a more recent case study of British urban success on a global scale. London, if not thought of in the terms of other cities in the post-war period, was at one point certainly seen as a failure. It isn't today. It is arguably the most vibrant, multicultural and successful city in the world. Using data on house prices and transport investment (and trying hard not to over infer) we can trace the journey of the capital from failure to pre-eminent success.

To start with, the journey of the London economy's renaissance is a long one, and it doesn't begin with the Olympics, or even with Canary Wharf and the policies of financial deregulation in the 1980s. In fact, on one reading, the origins of London's renaissance can be seen in the last gasp of old-fashioned social democracy in the late 1960s and 1970s.

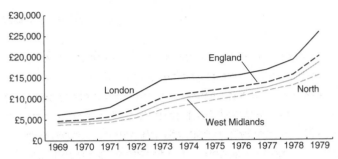

Figure 1. Simple average house prices 1969–79.

Even in 1969 London house prices were higher than those in the North. A decade later, before Margaret Thatcher had entered office, the trend of London pulling away from the North was already well established and has never really changed since. But looking at some of the big events that shaped the London we see today, the number of major transport (and other) intitiatives, and the centrality of government in each of them, is really quite arresting, as illustrated in figure 2. How important in this story, one wonders, was the impact of the Victoria Line opening in 1968, or the Jubilee Line a decade or so later?

The twenty years that separate the opening of the Jubilee Line in 1979 and its extension in 1999 were a period of remarkable growth in the economy of the city. This tube line, the development of Canary Wharf and the Docklands Light Railway, the big bang in the city and the opening of the Channel Tunnel rail link with direct services to Waterloo in 1994, to name but a few of the most obvious developments, all contributed to the flowering of London's potential, the growth in its population and the massive increase in house prices seen in the chart. The gap is widening relentlessly, and all of this is before the £15 billion investment in Crossrail starts to pay off.

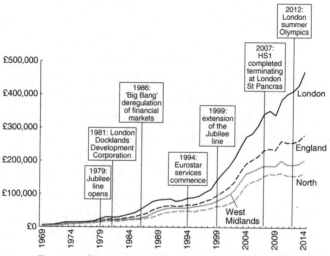

Figure 2. Simple average house prices 1969–2014.

The implication of this and of research on the New Deal in 1930s America,[64] is that patience will be needed in building the Northern Powerhouse, the Midlands Engine and their constituent cities. The foundations of London's renaissance are nearly fifty years old and not just the product of Thatcherism in the 1980s. City building takes a very long time. Investment in the right things, at scale and for a very long time is what matters.

Scale matters

It is almost impossible to provide even rough estimates of the sums involved in London's renaissance. But even once the scale of London's economy and its roles as the growth engine of the nation and a global visitor attraction are taken into account, the disparity between the billions of serial annual investment in London and what is on the table for other cities elsewhere is large indeed. One illustration of this is that the cost of station refurbishment of just two (albeit large) London underground stations at Bank and Victoria, at over £1.2 billion, would have funded much of the creation of the original Manchester Metrolink system: track, trains and signalling. Sustaining growth in London isn't cheap. Creating the conditions for it in the North, the Midlands and elsewhere won't be either.

Cities built our electricity, gas and water systems. They built aqueducts, canals and airports to meet the challenges of previous eras. The GVA gaps in our cities are not going to be filled by the small projects with which too many cities seem fixated. We need to build on positive evaluations of smaller-scale initiatives in transport and broadband.[65] Transformational projects in these areas, in infrastructure and town centre rebuilding, are all large and expensive projects if done at scale, and in most places are fundable and economic-value enhancing if they are approached correctly. Too many cities don't have a sharply honed view of the investments they need to raise their growth, or how to go about them. That has got to change. Taking a look at London's approach would be a good starting point.

On the human capital side, skills academies, provision for under-5s and support for innovation and its absorption into business should all be considered for public and private funding. Now is not a time for cities to shy away from thinking big. My colleagues at Metro Dynamics have shown how very different places can grow. In her work on what makes places magnetic to talent, Caroline Haynes set out to demonstrate that every place has an ability to be an attractor.[66] The key is in starting with an evidenced view of what the place is and has going for it. Then there is the vexed question of how to attract investment over and above the usual round of exhibitions – the key, here, which is too often overlooked, is offering viable projects at large enough scale to attract institutional investment. To achieve this, there is much scope to build on the North West Evergreen Fund, which created a pipeline of viable projects suitable for investment by the European Investment Bank and others – projects that on their own might never have attracted investment.[67]

Long-term vision

London has patently become a very successful place. Its problem is that its very success, allied to restrictive planning policies and inadequate housebuilding, have conspired to render large parts of the city and the more attractive parts of the towns in the surrounding regions unaffordable to all but the wealthiest people. At least part of the reason for this has been the economic conversion of London from being a city significantly dependent on manufacturing to being pre-eminent in services: a journey that other cities in the UK are starting, and will need, to take, even if industrial policy is successful. This is because the likelihood is low that any industrial policy can recreate anything like the tightly bonded and geographically closely located communities of mills and mines, with the populations who depended on them. It was this proximity that made these places, and the loss of jobs that has unmade them, leaving a range of problematic legacy issues, none more important than a tradition in which education played a relatively low role. As we have seen, education has become more important over time, with decent school qualifications a prerequisite for the majority of jobs. But poor schools don't just affect individuals, they blight places too – they are a key blocker in the process of helping places adjust following the loss of industry.

So even as policy does everything that can be done to create local employment, it is vital that cities and boroughs within cities look much more closely and critically at the legacy, positive and negative, of their past, focusing on what would make their location, and every neighbourhood in it, a place that people would choose to live and work in. Schools and parks are likely to be important. Housing mix is too. It is important to offer people real choices: to live in housing types and locations that will attract a mix of population types. Every borough has town centres and anchor institutions in education, culture and health that play a vital role to improve the "stickiness" of the place. These play to the strengths and opportunities each has, ameliorating weaknesses. Even if in-borough jobs may be a lower priority than hitherto, the market does and will continue to throw up inward investment opportunities for every city. The imperative is that opportunities for employment are seized, with proactive site development and planning, but more important is that places start to reimagine, with a very long-term vision, what they are and can be – this may, initially at least, be less about industry and commerce than hitherto.

Beyond the economy

Britain's cities have performed well in the last twenty years but, as the preceding analysis has served to show, we need to rethink them if we are to grow them: to shrink the gap between London's performance and that of other, larger, cities by growing the latter. The economic data only tell part of the story though. They offer some clear pointers. But to many, there remains a plausibility gap between what our great cities are now and what they would need to be to achieve the goal of having more world-class cities. Closing that gap is the aim of the ideas set out in the final part of this book. There were societal factors at play in the making and unmaking of British cities. We can learn from these too, positive and negative alike. So in looking at where we go next, to parallel this economic story, we need to look at the politics, governance and culture of cities in the UK. This is the subject of the next chapter.

Chapter 2

The social and political life of cities

The role of place and political culture in economies

In the globalized economy firms seek out the best places to make and sell. Their choices depend on economic factors but these are influenced by constitutional settlements and company law, which mediate the immensely liberating and destructive power of the market. Civil law jurisdictions tend to embed 'public duties' and responsibilities more rigorously than the codification of common law principles in English company law.[68] The continental approach also gives rise to statutory chambers of commerce and stronger local business organizations. In many countries the status of place is recognized in constitutional law too: cities and regions have powers that the national state simply cannot override, and many cities therefore have the power base from which to create unique business environments. For example, in the US there is a legacy of banking laws that until relatively recently prohibited out-of-state lending, alongside a strong vibrant civic culture resulting from being a continental federal nation.

Of course people and businesses are closely bound to specific places in the UK too. But the political, legal and social context in the UK is, by comparison with most countries, a less codified affair. The legacy of empire has also given British capitalism a particularly internationally oriented form. The absence of a written British constitution means that parliament can abolish or create pretty much any other part of the state with a majority of just one vote in the House of Commons. And the traditions of corporatist engagement between businesses and their workers or place, e.g. through workers' councils found in some of our more successful competitor nations (and some weaker ones), are absent. Indeed, the liberalism of the last decades has precisely defined itself against a supposedly failed earlier British corporatism. Surely these issues are not unimportant in a discussion of cities. And if the economic story of British cities told in chapter 1 is one of rising and declining places, we need to look to these institutional and other non-market foundations in order to understand more fully how these factors affect the fortunes of cities.

Polymaths and renaissance

In the minds of critics in the nineteenth century and since was the notion that cities and the industrial culture that spawned them were the creations of amoral profiteers – the dark side of Enlightenment rationalism: utilitarian and devoid of intrinsic human value.

One eminent historian of Britain's early industrial culture, Eric Evans, holds his profession guilty of having 'found the entrepreneur an ideologically unsympathetic subject' and of having 'either neglected or caricatured him'. He goes on to argue that, in fact:

> The sheer range of tasks performed by the factory masters and industrial capitalists of the period is staggering. It is a nice irony that while factory organization and discipline depended upon specialization of function among the work-force those who ran the firms were polymaths.[69]

If this is true – and any visit to an early mill reveals a level of organizational and mechanical complexity that lends credence to it – those who laid the foundations of modern urban life were closer to the ideal of the renaissance man than many historians have suggested. Enterprising the industrial pioneers most certainly were, but from the outset they were creative, organized and talented people.

A second renaissance? How cities perceived themselves

Time and time again histories of this period draw on the extensive wealth of material from nineteenth-century writers, politicians and industrialists. This material sought to draw lessons from antiquity and the Renaissance for what was underway in their Britain. Just as Athens started as a trading centre, blossoming into a creative force and the model of democracy, the moderns saw the need to push the boundaries of their endeavour. In 1844 Benjamin Disraeli commended Manchester for creating 'a great mercantile emporium' but noted 'an irresistible yearning for intellectual refinement' too. Having already built an athenaeum in Manchester (far from the only city to do so), they needed to go further, following the Athenian precedent, he said, to 'understand how business and commerce need never be an obstacle to intellectual and cultural advancement'.[70] Disraeli went further still, in his novel *Coningsby*:

> What Art was to the ancient world, Science is to the modern: the distinctive faculty. In the minds of men the useful has succeeded to the beautiful. Instead of the city of the Violet Crown, a Lancashire village has expanded into a mighty region of factories and warehouses. Yet rightly understood, Manchester is as great a human exploit as Athens.

> The inhabitants indeed are not as impressed with their idiosyncrasy as the countrymen of Pericles and Phidias. They do not fully comprehend the position which they occupy. It is the philosopher alone who can comprehend the inconceivable grandeur of Manchester, and the immensity of its future.[71]

I am not sure nineteenth-century Mancunians, or indeed other Britons, ever really understood the global significance of what was happening in British cities in this period or what this would mean for the cities themselves. Nonetheless, this was the moment when civic pride was burgeoning – a fact that leaps from the pages of Tristram Hunt's elegant account in *Building Jerusalem*. He quotes the chairman of the Manchester athenaeum, who saw the gap of 2000 years between the fall of Athens and the rise of his own city's institution in its name as an assertion that Manchester was in some sense picking up where the Athenians had left off.

The Victorian cities soon looked increasingly to a more recent urban renaissance for inspiration: Italy between the fourteenth and sixteenth centuries. In fact, if Manchester and the other cities saw themselves as emulating any city, it was Florence, whose commercial prowess was bettered only by its art. Perhaps ironically, given the limited role of government in Manchester and the consequences of this fact (considered later), history speaks of Britons of the time greatly admiring the traditions of Florentine self-government, sustained by the industrious middle class. This, it was argued, was the seedbed from which so many artistic flowers were to grow. Admiration for Florence also had an architectural impact on the cities, with many of the warehouses of Britain's cities being modelled on the grand palazzi of renaissance Florence, one of the finest being James Watt's warehouse on Portland Street in Manchester, which now hosts the not-so-grand Britannia Hotel.

A comparison with Venice is more valuable still. Venice (unlike Florence) was a new city, with a seemingly unfavourable location turned to advantage by people much like those in Northern England. Venice was, therefore, not a city with deep roots in an old culture but was formed by its people, who were migrants in the manner of ours. Venice was a city so powerful and unruly that the entire Republic was excommunicated by the Pope. Religious freedom was key to modern British cities. Venice was also a city that revolutionized a great many of the industries of its time. From printing and publishing to glass to banking, Venetian innovation and commercial acumen were a model for later cities. And Venice gave British cities the model for many of their very finest buildings: from the Wool Exchange in Bradford to the City Museum and Library in Bristol and a host of buildings including the Reform Club in Manchester. The more closely you look at British cities, the more credible is the argument that for a period, in the early to mid nineteenth century, they were building something consciously modelled on these two great urban forebears (although their independence and glory years lasted longer: better measured in centuries than decades).

So if the scale of ambition in Victorian cities was great but their period of glory so short, what can a brief survey of their cultural and political life tell us about their rise and fall?

Religious freedom and the impact on cities

Religious freedom is a relatively modern notion. Britain's bloody religious history meant that, even after the legal introduction of religious tolerance, it wasn't possible for anyone but Anglicans to hold high public office, or even to attend university, until quite late in the nineteenth century. Yet in none of the main cities was Anglicanism a majority, with Nonconformists making up an absolute majority of religious attendees in Bradford, Leeds, Oldham, Wolverhampton and Sheffield and close to a majority in Birmingham, Manchester, Salford and Newcastle, where Roman Catholics were also to be found in large numbers.[72]

So cities developed their own 'subcultures'. The merchants who had built the nonconformist chapels in the pre-industrial period were fundamental to the very creation of the Industrial Revolution.[73] The new industrial towns and cities were a model for what Robert Putnam[74] would later see as having strongly bonded social capital, which is so vital in the development and sustenance of successful communities. The chapels and Sunday Schools and the communities they spawned were fundamental in creating the innovative milieu of nineteenth-century cities.

Nonconformism formed the backbone of the political movements in the industrial cities, providing many of the most vocal political leaders (by instinct and party affiliation very largely Liberal) and civic officials too. Many, if not most, of the great entrepreneurs of the period were not Anglican either. The education that Nonconformists sponsored for their children was practically focused, with more 'sound training in the commercial arts' and in science than was the case with conformists. Given all of this, it should come as no surprise that Nonconformism played a key role in development in innovation. Eric Evans again:

> Dissenters played a leading role in the expansion of scientific knowledge, reflected in the work of the Royal Society in London and leading provincial organisations like the Literary and Philosophical Societies or Birmingham's famous Lunar Society... The links between science, drawing heavily on the new European learning, and technology probably have never been closer.[75]

Perhaps there is no better symbol of the role of religious Nonconformism, education and scientific endeavour in urban Britain than the University of Manchester, which was partly established as Owens College in 1851 through the legacy of the merchant John Owens. He was determined to establish a college where neither the staff nor the students had to satisfy any religious requirement. As in other places and at other times, religious tolerance in Britain – in London and in some of the Northern cities – meant that Jews, too, could live and work in peace. And so they did, with one account of Manchester arguing that the Christian religious culture of Nonconformism, striving for upward mobility and social acceptance, was very well aligned with that of the Jewish population.[76]

So their religious character gave the cities a strong moral purpose, underpinned by a distinctive religious culture that shaped, and provided vocal support for, the creation and sustenance of the fabric of civic life, supporting the wave of nineteenth-century economic progress. Cities were not the amoral cesspits often described and which greatly offended Victorian sensibilities. But they formed a counterpoint to the rural idyll (which for most working people was illusory anyway) and they fuelled the town and country rivalries that echo through literature and culture. Yet with rising prosperity came a decline in religious practice. The bonds of community and trust loosened, while the easing of religious restrictions and the triumph of consumerism also played a role in ensuring that within a very few generations, the legacy of religion in British cities was largely in its institutions – its universities, businesses and chapels – rather than in the people themselves.

Science, technology and a culture of learning in cities

Despite their civic ideals, the charge of philistinism hung over Britain's industrial cities as they grew. It led them to seek to define themselves in an artistic sense. But the charge was untrue in the first place. The learned societies described above were no add-on or late innovation. In nearly every major industrial city, they either prefigured or paralleled the very early days of industrialism, as Asa Briggs observes:

> The Literary and Philosophical Societies were proud of their role as the local cultural élite. Their presence or absence in these nineteenth century cities... was of considerable cultural and civic importance. Manchester's Society came into existence in 1781, Newcastle's in 1793, Liverpool's in 1812. Leeds founded its Society in 1819, Sheffield three years later.[77]

Each city had its own combination of institutions, which in Manchester included, alongside the Lit and Phil, the Portico Library, established in 1806 with Mark Roget (of *Roget's Thesaurus*) as its secretary. Elizabeth Gaskell was a regular patron and her husband William was its long serving chairman. Manchester Statistical Society was founded in 1833 and was the first in Britain established with the firm purpose of studying social problems systematically by collecting statistics. In 1821 a Natural History Society was created in the city, followed by the Royal Manchester Institution and a whole host of others. The Victorian cities organized themselves in a manner that lent itself to scientific discovery and innovation: that is to say, to the practical application of new ideas. They were determined to see these endeavours rooted in and contributing to the intellectual life of the rapidly changing world they were playing a major role in shaping.

But if these learned institutions were established for the creation of knowledge, there were also innovations in how knowledge, so created, would be shared with working people to enable them to learn the skills needed in the new world. These were the Mechanics' Institutes and the like, which sprung up in cities across the country and were subsequently taken up across the English-speaking world.

Urban political movements

The roll-call of political movements in nineteenth-century cities is as impressive as that of intellectual and scientific institutions. Here, too, British cities can legitimately claim to have been the forge in which political modernity was created.

The accomplishments of the Anti-Corn Law League are remarkable. The origins of the Corn Laws lie in a collapse in grain prices following the end of the Napoleonic wars and pressure from landowners for support. But by the 1830s, high grain prices during an economic downturn were having a devastating impact on the emerging cities. This led to the formation in 1839 in Manchester of the Anti-Corn Law League, whose aim from the outset was to relieve the plight of the working population and to assist business. The argument was that a reduction in tariffs would reduce prices, help feed people (and thereby reduce upward pressure on wages) and increase demand for British-manufactured products in the corn-exporting countries.

The league was a success in three senses. First, in 1846 the Corn Laws were repealed, so that imports rose and grain prices fell. Second, and arguably more importantly, a new political movement had brought together the interests of middle-class businesspeople and workers, successfully challenging the vice-like grip of the landed aristocracy on parliament. Third, a number of the movement's leaders, including John Bright and Richard Cobden, went on to become powerful players in the new Liberal politics of the cities and the country. This split the Conservative party in the process and provided a key staging point in the battle between conservatism and liberalism that would dominate national politics for decades thereafter.

Workers may have benefited from the middle-class leadership of the free trade movement, but they also played a critical role in movements of their own. Robert Owen, the Scottish mill owner, had led the way, but it was the Rochdale Pioneers (formed in 1844) who established a cooperative movement to provide reasonably priced, high-quality and, above all, unadulterated goods to working people. This eventually led to the creation of the Co-operative Group, which still plays an important role in British food retailing.

Trade Unionism too has very urban roots. The People's Charter of 1838 was driven by the London Working Men's Association, with other urban centres playing a key role in agitating for the 1842 General Strike. The Chartist Movement was defeated in 1848 with mass arrests, civil violence and the threat of military intervention. But it was the antecedent of the modern Trade Union movement. Later, the cause of women's suffrage was taken forward via the creation of the Women's Social and Political Union, based in Manchester. The Independent Labour Party was created at a meeting held in Bradford, and Salford saw the creation of the Vegetarian Society.

Political movements of both a liberal and socialist orientation, the development of both middle class and working class leadership, and the growth of both identity and interest politics were all central features of the great Victorian cities. Cities were vibrant polities whose mass media of the time – local newspapers – abounded and thrived. Some of them, such as the *Manchester Guardian*, were also to become significant on the national and international stage. However, even though the Anti-Corn Law League drew nine-tenths of its funds from the Manchester district, its headquarters were moved to London before the Corn Laws were repealed, in the early 1840s. The trade unions that emerged in the 1850s and onwards, like the Anti-Corn Law League, were highly organized national bodies, many of which were centred in London. The *Manchester Guardian* dropped the 'Manchester' in 1959, moving its headquarters to London five years later. Had all of these developments happened in the twentieth century, the argument that they were a consequence of the failure of our economic system in the cities would seem reasonable. However, many moves happened when the industrial cities were still very much in their heyday. Did these things happen because of something about the cities, or was it rather the centralizing pull of a powerful national polity? The centre of gravity of the UK as measured by the location of the middle class is probably one key factor. For example, in 1912 London and the Home Counties are estimated to have held just over a fifth of the country's population but about half of its middle class.[78] Was the failure of the cities to grow a bigger middle class part of the explanation for political centralization? Possibly, but governance may have been more important still.

The governance of cities

Viewed through the eyes and expectations of the early twenty-first century, it is quite easy when we look at the issue of political governance to see how the dynamism so apparent in the cities in the period up to the 1850s slipped away. This is where Manchester and the cotton pioneer cities, with the benefit of hindsight, look to have created a model of British political economy that has not served the country well, and which contrasts sharply with our international comparators.

Following the Reform Act of 1832, which dealt with the worst excesses of the Rotten Boroughs,[79] in 1835 came the Municipal Corporations Act, which created a new framework for local government. Manchester Corporation was created three years later, receiving city status in 1853. In other words, the Anti-Corn Law League, the major political movement with which the city is most associated, was formed at the same time as its most basic form of elected local government, and years before it became a city. This is no coincidence. It speaks to the extent to which Manchester and other industrial cities were formed by business, with political governance catching up considerably later.

If the aim of Cobden and others had been to create a lasting urban political culture, it didn't work. On one level this is a harsh judgement, for unlike, say, the former Hanseatic cities, and other cities elsewhere in Europe, Britain's had no constitutional rights to protect their interests. Manchester and the other Municipal Corporations were the creations of parliament. The 1835 Act was among the first of many examples in the nineteenth century of national inquiry leading to national policy to deliver local outcomes in cities. One striking example is the management of public health.

The challenge of public health

The combination of rapid population growth, low incomes and very limited government left all the early Victorian cities in a public health crisis. This lasted for decades as the cities simply failed to cope with the needs of their ever-expanding populations:

> The most beneficent central or local administration could not have kept pace with the unstructured influx [of people]; the prevailing ethos among Britain's early-nineteenth century legislators eschewed planning and intervention. In consequence the early industrial cities, whether factory or workshop based, became overcrowded, filthy, insanitary breeding grounds for disease, squalor and degradation. People flocked to them because they offered work but the social costs were enormous.[80]

Child mortality rocketed, with over 50% of children in 1830s Manchester and Sheffield failing to reach their fifth birthday, a situation brought about by poor sanitation and poor-quality and overcrowded housing. In 1841 life expectancy at birth was 26.6 years in Manchester, 28.1 years for Liverpool and 27 years in Glasgow, representing both a reversal in previous gains and increases in health inequalities.[81] As the public health problems of the towns and cities mounted, the middle classes moved out, creating the patterns of residential and epidemiological segregation and differentiation that still characterize many urban areas. Little meaningful reform of housing and public health originated in the cities before or after the 1835 legislation.

If the Victorian cities could be forgiven for their inability to manage the problems of industrialization in the early period of their existence, the failure to do so decades later is both an indictment of the cities themselves and a factor in the creation of conditions that encouraged national government to step in later in the century:

> The Sanitary Commission of 1869 to 1871, which collected ample evidence concerning the ignorance, petty jealousies and unwillingness to spend money of the mid-Victorian Local Boards of Health, was the prelude to the setting up of the Local Government Board in 1871, the Public Health Act of 1872, the comprehensive Public Health Act of 1875, which divided the country into urban and rural sanitary districts with clearly defined duties, and the Artisans' and Labourers' Dwellings Improvement Act of the same year.[82]

In other words, national government decided it had to step in to rectify the failings of urban public administrations. The weakening over time of the city-led process of development lay in the cities' own failure to grapple with their most pressing problems. As Tristram Hunt argues, the role of city government was very limited in these key areas of policy, even some years after incorporation:

> By the 1860s there was a festering impatience with the classic, Victorian way of doing things: of voluntarism, civic association and muddling through. Since the 1835 Municipal

Corporation Act, local councils had been placed in nominal charge of their towns and cities and yet very little seemed to have been achieved by them. Instead it was the churches, business leaders and friendly societies which had run the city.[83]

The pioneer cities had shown themselves to be unwilling to deal, or incapable of dealing, with a great many of the worst problems created by their rapid development. For sure the cities eventually sought to rectify the problem with the Municipal Gospel of Joseph Chamberlain in Birmingham and the growth of municipal socialism in Glasgow and London, and the cotton pioneers and others invested massively in the creation of modern sanitation, gas and electricity.[84] Yet these achievements in public service were not enough to avert the strong impulse of central government to intervene.

The cities did eventually rise to the challenge, but the political initiative had been lost at a point when they still had the economic power to strike a different political bargain with an emergent national state. So much of the early freedom of cities, with their ability to regulate, was sacrificed as national government had had to intervene on issue after issue to deal with their manifest problems. Public policy, even in the biggest cities, became the business of central government. This helped to both create and cement the striking centralization of political power in Britain.

The culture of cities

The leaders of Victorian cities had great hopes, then, for their cultural endeavour. Did they deliver on them? The results are mixed.

The sternest test is whether we can see, with a hundred years' hindsight, if culture made a discernible and enduring contribution to the legacy of the places themselves and to their standing in the wider world. Viewed through this lens, Victorian cities do not fare so well, London excepted.

Perhaps because, as essentially new places, industrial cities had little heritage in high art (something for which they were mocked mercilessly), they tended to look back to antiquity and the Renaissance, though Manchester took its cue from London too. It built on the Great Exhibition of 1851 when, six years later, it chose to host the Art Treasures Exhibition: a first, as it was devoted entirely to art. As well as establishing the institutions described above, the nouveaux riches of the city bought art on a large scale, yet this was usually as active and generous sponsors of London-based artists, such as the Pre-Raphaelites.[85] Take the example of William Fairbairn, a member of the organizing committee of the Arts Treasures Exhibition and a great supporter of the Pre-Raphaelites, who commissioned extensively from the London-based William Holman Hunt. Though he succeeded in his quest to secure the opening of what is now the Manchester

City Art Gallery, by way of local artistic legacy he left little more than portraiture. Even the great town halls across the north of England, and the art decorating them, served to fund cultural production elsewhere.

Perhaps the most important countervailing institutional development during this period was the development of the Manchester School of Design, established in 1838 at the same time as what is now the Royal College of Art in London, both formed (along with others) in response to an 1836 Parliamentary Select Committee report that recommended the creation of design schools to improve the skills of British workers and hence the quality of the nation's design and manufacture.[86] This later became the Manchester School of Art, led by Walter Crane and the home of Adolphe Valette, who taught L. S. Lowry at the school long after the rot of urban decline had set in, and too late to play a role in stopping it.

THE MUSICAL LIFE OF CITIES

London had always been a major musical centre, dominating the country even late in the industrial period, with ten times the number of musicians of any other city.[87] Only Newcastle among the industrial cities had, courtesy of Charles Avison, a strong prior tradition of musical production, but even this did not endure.[88]

Little 'art music' seems to have been written in the industrial cities, and still less of it was played by resident professional musicians. But studies of working class culture find ample evidence of cultural literacy and musical activity in working class households throughout the nineteenth century and deep into the twentieth. Its legacy – of brass bands in England and the Welsh choral tradition – live on to this day. If the life of cultural production in British cities didn't reach the heights of creative exploration elsewhere, there is little to suggest that this was in any way a reflection of the working people who lived there.[89] Yet, as with art, where strong institutions were created there is legacy.

In respect of art music, Manchester's story illustrates the picture well. The Gentlemen's Concerts had been a feature of the city since the 1760s. It was one of their organizers, Hermann Leo, who persuaded Charles Hallé to move to Britain in 1848. The result was the Hallé Orchestra, formed nine years later. In 1893, under Hallé's leadership, the Royal Manchester College of Music was established; this was followed, in 1920, by the Northern School of Music; and then, in 1973, the two merged to form the Royal Northern College of Music. Leo, Hallé and others prominent in Manchester music were ethnic Germans. Their legacy, uniquely among the Northern cities, was a substantial teaching facility and an orchestra of renown, providing the premiere of

Elgar's First Symphony, for example, and the UK premieres of works by the likes of Gluck, Mozart, Berlioz and Tchaikovsky. This institution has endured and Manchester has been on the map ever since.

In most other cities, like a passing storm, London-based or international musical talent came and went, leaving little impact. Manchester created its own institutions to embody and steward the culture the city wanted to see across generations. Others cities did too but, as in Manchester, this tended to happen quite late in the process of industrialization, while some were more reliant on festivals.[90] Manchester's legacy in music is similar to its legacy in science, where strong institutions have stood the city in good stead across generations. The rub, in music at least, is that the city did not produce a distinctive musical style until after the German locals' influence on Manchester's music had waned. The 'New Manchester Music' of Harrison Birtwhistle and Peter Maxwell Davies was very much part of a modernist cultural revolution that, almost by design, alienated and excluded a more conservative working class musical audience, which was by then turning its attention to the easy virtues of radio and television; one among many such links between working class culture and high art had been lost, adding to the residential separation and the differences in educational and health outcomes described earlier.[91]

So why did British cities fade as polities?

The first chapter of this book concluded that institutional design was an important part of the story of cities' rise and decline. So too is the political case considered above. In both cases, the amazing achievements of our system of cities looks to have been undermined by low levels of adaptability to change: characterized by weak institutions that, like their economies and politics, are at least in part a product of the places themselves.

One conclusion to be drawn is that the fall of British cities was in part because their institutional weakness contributed to their inflexibility and their failure to adapt. Institutions, when they work well, mediate change, accelerating the beneficial effects of the market when that makes sense, and providing a bulwark against the market elsewhere. Education and health inequalities were hard wired into cities from the outset, via weak governance, with little to counter their debilitating effects; the lack of institutions, or their late development in the case of culture, was a contributory factor in an economic model that valued human capital too little and made less use of financial capital too. In these domains, institutions and networks (private or public) – which in other jurisdictions buttress the power of individuals and markets – seem either never to have existed or have failed to endure. So the question arises: why didn't the cities develop more and stronger institutions?

This is an impossible question to answer. The cities certainly had too much confidence in the infallibility of their businesses and their success in the markets in which their world domination was to be fleeting. Perhaps, too, there was an element of hubris. But even revolutionary Manchester was up against something more powerful: British cultural snobbery.

Snobbery and our attitude to cities

As a nation, we don't love our cities. We don't think of ourselves as an urban people. In April 1993, speaking to the Conservative Group for Europe, Prime Minister John Major sought to evoke a sprit of 'British-ness'. The vision he conjured up was of shaded cricket greens, warm beer, suburbs and, quoting George Orwell, 'old maids bicycling to Holy Communion through the morning mist' – and this from a South Londoner who found his version of paradise in rural Cambridgeshire.[92] This goes deep. Take a look at three quintessentially British items: William Blake's *Jerusalem*, our quasi-national anthem; Charles Dickens's *Hard Times*, one of our most treasured books; and our passports, one of our most important national documents.

Interpretations of William Blake's words in his poem *Jerusalem* range widely but, to most people, I suspect, his depiction of 'dark satanic mills' is an image that is the very opposite of the Jerusalem he would have seen built. As he wrote in the early nineteenth century, Britain's urban development was really gathering steam and he shared the widespread revulsion against it.

One person who very much felt the revulsion towards the cities of mid-Victorian Britain was Charles Dickens. In his depiction of Coketown in *Hard Times* – a place of slums and workhouses, characterized by the grim utilitarianism of the teacher Thomas Gradgrind – Dickens set out to condemn the very nature of the modern industrial city: not just the human misery it created at that time, but the elevation of the pursuit of profit into a system that both created it and worshipped it on such a large scale.

Of course Dickens and Blake both wrote in the nineteenth century. What of today? The passport issued in the years before 2016 was described by the then head of the Passport Office as seeking to represent the scenic aspects of Britain. It contains arcadian images of cliffs, formal parks, rivers and the like. Even the canal is rural. Not a single scene is urban. Blogging in the *London Review of Books* one commentator at the time observed:

> The imagery presents a conservative, not to say nostalgic, view of Britain as a cloudy, often wet country of landscape and built heritage... Apart from one glance at the fishing industry... there is no evidence of any industry or occupation that our futures might depend on. The complete absence of any image of a city – even an old city – is to represent a Britain that most passport-holders may visit from time to time, but don't live in.[93]

These are not isolated examples but form part of a clear picture of a deeply held view of cities in the UK. This is not a wholly British issue. As Ed Glaeser observes, implicit anti-urban policy in the US embodies the spirit of Thomas Jefferson and would find support from the likes of Mahatma Ghandi.[94] But our anti-urban bias is maybe deeper and older still, with one sixteenth-century traveller noting that 'among the English nobles think it is shameful to live in towns; they reside in the country, withdrawn among woods and pastures'.[95]

As Tristram Hunt reminds us, the evils of the city were juxtaposed against rustic virtue even as long ago as in the bible's tale of Sodom and Gomorrah – something that has been echoed in the speeches of contemporary clerics who have drawn comparisons.[96] Perhaps the easy virtues of cities are unchristian. They certainly came to be seen as un-British. Writing decades later, this is how the English author J. B. Priestley came to view the Industrial Revolution:

> Most of us English still cherish an instinctive feeling that men come first and that machines should come a long way afterwards. It is true we were the first machine people, partly because we enjoy inventing machines – and still do – but the idea of serving machines did some injury to the English psyche. Yes of course the wages, the hours, the conditions were terrible, but there was something else, an instinctive resentment, that completed the black bitterness. *And it is with us yet.*[97]

Our view of our history is warped, divisive and deeply counterproductive to our national interest. The early modern cities of the UK created conditions of deep human misery, but it is very hard indeed to see how Britain could have become the country it is today – prosperous, diverse and culturally savvy – without the process of the Industrial Revolution and the creation of the cities and towns that gave birth to it. There is no return to the preindustrial age as we have the legacy of the Industrial Revolution in the very fabric of the country. But the urban revolution was a far from complete one in Britain. More than that, the adaptability and resilience of British class culture played a key role in embracing and, in the end, deflating Victorian urban industrial spirit.

Aristocracy and its effects on urban leadership

British cities are embedded in a national polity that had seen off the kind of revolutionary turmoil of eighteenth-century France. With less ease but eventual success it quelled the rise of Chartism, which might have resulted in the kind of revolutionary foment the rest of Europe experienced in 1848. Indeed, the response of the aristocracy to industrialization was part of that process. As noted earlier, landowners played a key role in the early investment in industrialization, thereby shaping it and, as importantly, providing a fixed focal point as the upper stratum in British life. A goal. That status was also a goal that many of those who made their money from industry chose to strive for. Martin Weiner describes the process as 'social absorption' in which the

> zeal for work, inventiveness, material production and money making gave way within the capitalist class to the more aristocratic interests of cultivated style, the pursuits of leisure, and political service.[98]

Hardly surprising, then, that the Grand Tour and the country mansion became common for many rich entrepreneurs, and a classical Oxbridge education became de rigeur for their offspring (something that has changed little since then). That people made these choices – and that so many did so by seeming to reject so much of what they were and what had made them – speaks to the issue we have with our urban identity: the sense of its inferiority and limitations with which so many Britons still seem to wrestle.

As one historian wrote, comparing the US with Britain, 'the best society of Philadelphia was trying to improve and glorify Philadelphia [while the] best society of Manchester was trying to get out of it'.[99] Richard Cobden, who unusually (having been born in Sussex in the South) made his life in Manchester (though he died in London), mourned that the 'spirit of feudalism' was 'rife and rampant', as those around him moved onwards and outwards.[100]

If those who made it in the cities were really trying to get out and to ensure that their children became something 'better' than they were, then Cobden was right. For him, aristocracy was the enemy of the civic culture, to the creation of which he devoted so much of his life. Civic culture has to be strong enough to break free of the shadow of past aristocracy while incorporating all that is good about it. Too much of our cities' economic drive lay in company owners whose children had less interest in the civic and religious ties that bonded them than did their parents. The new cities, especially those of the revolutionary cottonopolis that came to dominate British industrial culture, also had too little of the glue of business associations and the the legacy of guilds and chambers of commerce that characterized other competitor countries, looking after the long-term interests of business and ensuring a supply of people and innovation to keep up momentum.

Chapter 3

Centralization, decline and renewal

The creeping political centralization of Britain

There was nothing inevitable about the centralization of the British state, and this was even more true when it came to civic life than it was with the economy. Indeed, until the 1970s local government remained powerful, the deliverer of a great many public services, even if by this time the political and economic power of the cities as polities had waned greatly. But there is little doubt that the centralizing tendencies of the national state played an essential role. The litany of national commissions and the legislation to which they give rise, as described earlier, is testament enough to that. But local government lost some key battles along the way too: none more important that that over the National Health Service (NHS).

There is a double irony in the story of the NHS from the point of view of cities. The first is that when William Beveridge set about his reforms, much of the provision he saw was the creation of local, and very often city, government. Although Beveridge was silent on what form what we now know as the NHS should take in the post-war implementation of his proposals, the balance of argument was against a new national bureaucracy until Aneurin Bevan intervened. Bevan wanted a national system, and he won the argument. The second irony is that Bevan later came to regret his decision, lamenting in 1954 that he felt that the lack of an elected base for the health service was a weakness in the system, and advocating local government reorganization to give it the scale to manage the NHS – something that has not happened until very recently and even now in only one city.[101]

Immediately after World War II electricity was nationalized (1947), and two years later so was gas. In 1973 local responsibility for water was regionalized. Local government reorganization saw the creation of the Greater London Council and the metropolitan counties. Nationalization was centralization. But the real existential crisis that would play out in British cities occurred in the period leading up to and especially following the 1979 election of Margaret Thatcher.

The trauma started before 1979. The response to the sterling crisis of 1976 and the need for the British government to seek an IMF loan, the subsequent austerity programme and worsening industrial relations were all symptoms of a crisis that had been brewing for decades. Despite the best efforts of Peter Shore, whose 1977 White Paper on the inner cities was the first official recognition of the urban problem and even led to investment in urban renewal, post-war anti-urban policy continued to drain life from cities and into new and expanded towns, exacerbating the already powerful centrifugal power of the car-driven 'American age' economy.[102] Even more enthusiastic austerity after 1981 allied to a hike in sterling made matters a great deal worse, creating the perfect conditions for the collapse in the traditional industries of many towns and cities. The miners' strike of 1984 was in part precipitated by, and certainly helped to consolidate, the rapid shrinkage of the mining industry, while in terms of mass employment, the staple industries of most of the cities of the UK were all but wiped out.

Unsurprisingly, cities found themselves in the middle of the politics of this process, with very much more left-wing leaders taking over the reins of Labour councils and the rise of the Militant Tendency in a number of cities, best symbolized by Derek Hatton's Liverpool. This was a toxic combination. A Conservative national government with a highly laissez faire agenda and a missionary zeal for economic reform faced a more ideologically left-wing group of city leaders and trade unions prepared to use their leverage with the intention that while privatization may be what the government wanted, they would create civic socialism. The government's predictable response was to abolish some of local government (the Greater London Council and other metropolitan county councils) and systematically bypass the rest of it. Councils lost control of higher education (polytechnics), further education, housing and much of public transport. And through Urban Development Corporations many cities lost the initiative on the most basic civic function of city regeneration. Finally, local government finance was more or less nationalized through the creation of the 'poll tax', and its successor Council Tax, and the Uniform Business Rate.

A Conservative minister with strong one-nation instincts that led him to invest his time in cities was Michael Heseltine. The governments in which he served were active centralizers but his instincts were pro-city: to try to revive commercial property and other urban markets, working in close partnership with cities by the end of his tenure as deputy prime minister in 1997. Before we turn, finally, to the current renaissance of cities, a fitting way to end the story of decline is with Peter Hennessy's epic on the civil service, on Michael Heseltine and on the legacy with which he and every government since have been grappling. In virtually his only reference to cities Hennessy writes:

> On his Monday visits to Merseyside Michael Heseltine would acknowledge the grim reality that all the best efforts of his Merseyside Task Force would be more than offset when, at the stroke of a Chairman's pen in a multinational's boardroom far away from Liverpool or even from Britain, one of

the area's big employers would be closed down, another victim to the vagaries of the so-called 'branch economy'. Quite apart from such mega forces, a problem – relative economic decline in its starkest and most geographically specific form – which had taken, in some cases and some places, the best part of the century to develop its malign chemistry is not going to be put right in the life of a Parliament, however well conceived the antidotes coming out of the Whitehall policy units and committee rooms. As so often, the judgement has to be that without Whitehall's efforts and the disbursement of public money, matters would be even worse in the 'Giro towns' of the old industrial areas and in the 'underclass' pockets of the towns and cities of the relatively prosperous south-east. It is not an heroic epitaph – but it is virtuous one.[103]

What a journey our nation has travelled, from emulating Athens and Rome to sweetening the bitter pill of 'giro towns'[104] within a century or so. Hennessey is right that it takes more than a parliament to fix such deepseated problems, but he is at best only half right in his assertion that matters would have been worse without Whitehall's intervention. As the final part of this book shows, a great deal of policy on cities, most of it emanating from Whitehall, hasn't worked. It is far from obvious that empowered city leaders would have fared worse.

The end of centralization?

If the low point for British cities was one brought about by benign neglect, their stabilization and recovery, along with the rest of the country, has been, in part, the product of quite the opposite: a hyper-innovatory national government machine that has sought to intervene in every aspect of policy with the aim of securing high national standards. Alongside privatization under the Thatcher administrations was the development of a parallel form of interventionist regulation often termed New Public Management (NPM).[105] Initially in education and health, and then pretty much everywhere else too, and in a way that transcended party political boundaries (indeed, NPM is one of the key crossover policies between the Conservatives and New Labour), the state would create quasi-markets in which public service bodies would compete with each other or be regulated in order to drive performance improvement. There follows from this, naturally, the need for inspection, target setting and monitoring, and the creation of frameworks of control and reward. It has transformed much public policy and delivered very significant efficiency benefits too.[106] It has been an important means by which economies like ours (which want high European levels of public service with low American-style taxes) have been able to deliver more for less public money over a long period. It is far from perfect. By reducing much public policy to technocratic planning and review, it has squeezed the room for debate about the nature of policy and underplayed the interconnectedness of much health, education and other policy. That, in turn, has not helped the cause of cities, as it has consolidated a design feature of British public policy that cities, and indeed all local government, have wrestled with for generations.

The British state operates on a strong model of vertical accountability, from parliament going down to schools and hospitals. The Secretaries of State for health and education are accountable not to the prime minister but to parliament for the spending it grants them. Perhaps more than in most countries, a newly arriving minister feels a sense of personal responsibility to deliver on a powerful mandate that comes not from one person but from the country. Very often, local government – and especially in powerful cities – is in the way of spending ministers, their departments and their single-issue focus.

The welfare problem of many deprived cities is in large measure down to long-term unemployment and is concentrated in certain areas and in certain families with multiple problems. Here one often finds a challenging combination of poverty, poor education and skills, low labour market attachment, poor health (including mental health), problems of substance misuse and high rates of criminality. Typically, people in the poorest areas don't just die earlier, they spend an extra seventeen years of their shorter lives with a disability compared with those in the most affluent neighbourhoods.[107] The evidence, confirmed in the work of Sir Michael Marmot and others, is that the post-1945 welfare settlement, driven by large national functional bureaucracies, and this kind of managerialism have made things work less well than when the problem was fixing 'the five giants' identified by Beveridge. As the Manchester Independent Economic Review revealed,[108] during the longest period of growth since records began – with the highest ever increase in public spending in peacetime and with billions of pounds targeted over a thirty-year period towards reducing inequality and deprivation – little progress was made on reducing deprivation, and in some places it actually got worse.[109] While we don't know what would have happened had that spending not been made, the case that current policies are working is simply not borne out by evidence, pre- or post-austerity.

If the goals of high standards of public service to be delivered largely free at point of use are to be maintained, and within a level of tax spending with which the British people are comfortable, a rethink is needed. Not just in terms of how we deliver better outcomes from public services but about how we can better embrace the major societal challenges and opportunities that give rise to service needs. This is where cities should, and will, come into their own again.

The level of centralization in the British state is unhealthy. Nearly three in five Britons say they expect more from their politicians than they do from God.[110] No wonder national politicians feel the need to deliver on every issue under the sun. But they cannot. NPM regimes forcing public service organizations to compete with each other only work if you are prepared to close failing schools and hospitals. Ministers have found that difficult to deliver in practice while local residents, for good or ill, still seem to favour local provision even if it is demonstrably worse.

As a civil servant I was centrally involved in the creation of the System of Comprehensive Performance Assessments for local councils. This was designed both to bring about efficiencies in council performance and to reward, through devolution, those who succeeded. A panoply of controls was duly created and the system launched. But as with schools and hospitals, and unlike the market mechanisms on which the model is based, there was no automatic process by which those who failed would be removed. Ministers proved very reluctant indeed to stand down failing and bankrupt councils *pour encourager les autres*, in the way the threat of insolvency does to entrepreneurs. As in education and health, real achievements in outcomes were delivered but the effect was less transformational than we had hoped or expected. At the same time we tried devolution through other means too. There has been a string of initiatives including local public service agreements (LPSAs), local area agreements, multi-area agreements and statutory city regions: deals between the centre and the local producing what Sir Richard Leese once famously described as 'devolution-free devolution deals'. That there was no devolution is not an accident but another product of the way Whitehall is designed. I remember sitting in Cabinet Committee meetings with members poring over proposals for devolution through LPSAs. Minister after minister argued against even the most modest service devolution from their precious departmental spending budgets, citing cataclysm should national policy be devi-ated from. When, instead, they spoke as colleagues, ditching their ministerial briefs, the trade-offs involved seemed too complex for them to understand, let alone assess. This is because the centralized system is over-loaded with too much policy on too many non-central issues. Centralized British government has overreached itself on a monumental scale and is not functional. In policy and political terms it is a national monopoly, and like many other monopolies it has become inefficient. Ed Glaeser looked at it through the other end of the tele-scope but came to the same conclusion in the US:

> There is a lot to dislike in political systems that lodge too little power in local hands, but the answer isn't complete autonomy, either. When things work right, multiple layers of government – federal, state, and city – can check each other especially when different parties hold power at different layers.[111]

This is echoed by other writers such as Francis Fukay-ama, whose argument is that complex problems are best solved by those with highly delegated authority (which Whitehall finds difficult). Statebuilding, he argues, should be based on the principle of subsidiarity – something we find easier to discuss in a pan-European context than in an intra-British one.[112]

The argument often made, until quite recently, in relation to devolution was that there is an absence of evidence that local government could do it any better than central government. No wonder. In virtually no area of public policy has even the biggest city authority in the sixth biggest economy in the world the budgetary power to challenge the most centralized state in Europe: not even the great cities that created modern Britain. If Britain had the resources to carry on running services the way we do, or if it had new and compellingly models for how we can fix the great problems of our times, let alone rebalance the economy, perhaps the status quo would be an option. But we haven't, and it isn't. So while perhaps the case for devolution has yet to be fully established empirically, the case for change is undeniable.

Rays of hope

The hope for political decentralization in England does not come from the Labour government's failed experiment with regional devolution – an experiment in which I participated. That was seen off by a referendum in the North East that need never have taken place on a package of measures that didn't warrant it. The package had been weakened by a highly devolution-resistant Whitehall and was duly rejected by the people of the North East by an overwhelming majority.

The hope for devolution came in a 2009 Act of Parliament that created the first legal basis for devolution based on groups of local authorities. This legislation was strongly promoted by Greater Manchester, for whom the creation of a light-touch strategic authority in which the ten districts of the conurbation were constituent members seemed the logical next step in a twenty-year process of deepening collaboration. This answered a fundamentally important question. Prior to the creation of these new 'combined authorities' there was no pan-city region legal personality to which government could devolve, and no responsible government could devolve real powers to informal mechanisms of cooperation. 'Who is in charge?' was always the question from Westminster and Whitehall.

Today there are seven combined authorities covering some of the major city regions of the country. They are in charge. Each is a legal personality: a local authority to which power can, for the first time, be devolved at the city region level. It is a delicious irony that one of the first acts of the decidedly small-state local government minister in the coalition government in 2010, Eric Pickles, was to create a new layer of government: the Greater Manchester Combined Authority.

Steps to devolution

Greg Clark, the Minister for Cities after 2010, was the first to use the term 'licensed exceptions' for cities. This is what he wanted from the process of city deals that he instigated with the support of the Chancellor of the Exchequer, George Osborne, and Lord Heseltine. A total of eight first-wave city deals were signed, nearly all of them with areas developing combined authorities. These were bespoke deals with the most devolution going to the areas of the country that were showing ambition, creativity and the kind of organization needed to handle it. They were another modest but important step.

The game changer came out of nowhere. George Osborne had been thinking about his legacy for a while, emboldened by his reading of Robert Caro and his books on Lyndon Johnson, the (Democrat) American president, and Robert Moses, the 'powerbroker' who built New York.[13] The outcome was a speech Osborne gave in June 2014 during which he announced the notion of a Northern Powerhouse – evocative of the nineteenth-century cities described earlier – and invited cities to come forward with their proposals for devolution to help create it. Central to his vision were elected mayors for cities and regions, investment in transport and culture. He promised more serious devolution and made further significant steps towards delivering it. Unlike previously, there was no elaborate process. The first deal, again with Greater Manchester, was negotiated through Whitehall by Osborne and his advisers, with the raw power of HM Treasury being used to secure a loosening of Whitehall's grip on power in favour of cities in what has been likened to a smash-and-grab raid.[114]

After the 2015 election (and a manifesto commitment to devolution), cities and other groups of councils were invited to bring forward their proposals in the summer of 2015. When Osborne left office in the summer of 2016, ten devolution deals had been agreed, covering 16.1 million people, with the first directly elected metro mayors due in place in May 2017.

With these deals came further devolution, including in welfare to work and business as well as more devolution in skills and the first major devolution in transport, with the power to reregulate buses in many areas. There is a new mantra behind most of these deals: growth and reform. This means measures that will grow the business base economies and others that will reduce the costs of failure in public service provision. The deals are not massive. The National Audit Office estimate additional investment of £7.4 billion over thirty years, or £246.5 million pounds per year, compared with annual capital expenditure within the same areas of £4.4 billion.

A new era for cities

This is a new era for cities. They are growing again, and by 2017 some of our biggest cities will be run by elected metro mayors. Their very existence marks an important turning point. They will be a powerful voice, joining the Mayor of London and, on occasion, the first ministers of the devolved administrations in arguing their cause. This will be more so if the new metro mayors are credible figures on the national stage too. Andy Burnham – the runner-up in the Labour party's 2015 leadership election and a would-have-been future prime minister – was selected as Labour's candidate in Manchester. In the West Midlands, the Conservatives have chosen Andy Street, the outgoing CEO of virtually Britain's last untarnished business treasure, John Lewis. Both are nationally credible figures.

There is much more to be done to improve the governance of cities but there is an experiment underway in which local councils are being moulded into new ways of working together. This is making them look, in principle, more capable of answering the long-standing problems of British urban policy than the Whitehall system from which they are seeking devolution. And then there is 'the English question'. Even before the European referendum, the British body politic was unstable, with a nationalist Scotland far from settled. Now a second referendum looms. So long as the Kingdom remains United and the resources flow the way they do to Scotland, Wales and Northern Ireland, the messy compromise within the Union will be contested and the mayors of our metro cities will press the case at every turn for more devolution. Maybe this will create a different English constitutional settlement too. Perhaps most importantly of all, the vote to leave the European Union has revealed quite serious divisions within British society. These are not principally between urban and rural areas but there is a sense in the places most affected by industrial decline in the last forty years that enough is enough. A message has been sent to all mainstream politicians that it is time for action. If our national politics has expended all of its ammunition and the alternatives are populism and extremism of a kind that make UKIP look mainstream, cities start to look like a more attractive option for nurturing a sane and progressive politics.

Devolution (at the moment) is small beer in financial terms. It is early days. What parliament gives, so too parliament can take away. Devolved programmes and resources promised and agreed by George Osborne for welfare, skills and business have already been abolished or reduced. Moreover, neither Theresa May nor Philip Hammond seem as invested in the devolution project as David Cameron and George Osborne were. The same can be said of Labour's Jeremy Corbyn in relation to those who preceded him.

The context for devolution has changed too. The effects of long-term industrial change are being felt so widely, and with many of the conurbation core cities having voted to remain in the European Union, there may just be a sense that cities have had their time and attention: that it is time to spread the money around more. This, as we saw earlier, would be a weaker economic approach, given the importance of agglomeration in driving economic growth. It is not impossible, then, that devolution could go seriously awry in some cities. This possibility is made all the more likely by the fact that without an easing of austerity, some local authorities will be at the point where they can barely meet their statutory obligations let alone invest at the scale needed to build a new urban renaissance.

There is a long road ahead, then, before we will know if this really is a new era. But if we start with the view that a new era is both possible, based on the recently laid foundations, and necessary, because we need to find a better way to deliver the growth and reform our country needs in cities, then this is a good start. If we are mindful of the great achievements of our urban forebears, learning the lessons from what they and our national leaders got wrong or from where they fell short, we could achieve something that is more durable, with stronger markets, more successful businesses and business institutions supported by stronger city governance.

The book's final chapter sets out some ideas about how we can once again secure the high economic and political ground that our cities sought to create in the formative part of our story. But a failure to properly understand just how far our cities fell, why that happened and, moreover, how seemingly comfortable our country has been for so long with the status quo means we risk continuing to repeat the mistakes of the past. Peter Hennessey's view, quoted earlier, is not uncommon or even unusual. As a Treasury official concerned with government policy on cities, I recall being told several times not to worry: that the automatic stabilizer of expansionary welfare spending would ensure that cities didn't suffer too much in downturns. The automatic stabilizers are the state benefits paid to those in need in the 'giro town' jibe. I recently overheard a former member of the Bank of England's Monetary Policy Committee complaining that we have 'tried everything' in Burnley and 'nothing works'. Only a country that has never really understood or properly nurtured what it created during the Industrial Revolution – or one that has become so detached from it that it has in effect succumbed to a kind of societal amnesia – could take such views and allow them to hold over generations. The case I have made here is that both are true. This is the challenge we face in rebuilding urban Britain.

Chapter 4

An agenda for the future

Introduction

This book has explored the rising and falling fortunes of British cities and concluded that there are tentative but real grounds for optimism. The aim has been not just to outline what has happened but, within the limitations of imprecise data and in the absence of research in key areas, to seek to understand why this is so and what implications the past has for the future. The signs are that the future of Britain's cities hangs in the balance between a return to stagnation and further renewal. The recent move to devolve power to English cities is an important source of optimism. The cities themselves are waking up to the possibilities open to them. And Brexit is a challenge to which Britain, not least its cities, has yet to rise.

As US writers such as Bruce Katz and Benjamin Barbour have argued, in a world where the power of nation states is waning, city regions with powerful mayors have a powerful role to play.[115] How things happen is as important as what is done. But as work by the OECD's Programme on Local Economic and Employment Development has shown, city leadership is about more than mayors.[116] There are lessons here for the private sector as well as for city and national government. Many of the important issues I draw out here have been known to British policy makers for the last fifty or hundred years. Addressing them is often characterized as a choice between a liberal market approach and one that is based more on government intervention. While this is indeed an important choice, there is a more nuanced question about institutional design, and about getting the balance right between individual decision-making on the one hand and, on the other, securing collective agreement where this is most appropriate. Institutional design matters, and cities should be a hothouse for innovation in this area. This is neither easy nor, frankly, very British. It will be a challenge.

SIX PRINCIPLES FOR CITY DEVOLUTION

British public policy tends to be evolutionary. How might a revolution begin when it comes to cities? Some general principles might be a good starting point.

A presumption for devolution

A devolutionary ratchet is needed to overcome the centralizing tendency of recent decades, along with safeguards over how it works. Devolution and keeping power devolved within a framework of accountability should be the objective, with the boundaries of what is central and local remaining essentially contestable.

Devolution means devolution

Subject to meeting a test of capacity and probity, which ought to include the existence of a highly performing combined authority and a mayor, major cities should be free to seek devolution of any area of public spending that is not inherently national in nature. There should be a presumption in favour of devolution except where this would be likely to be against the national interest.

National standards

British people dislike postcode lotteries in public services even if they seem to accord undue respect to the national bureaucracies responsible for most of them. So, where the country as a whole has determined minimum outcome standards in health, education and other areas, these minima should bind devolved cities as they do existing providers – though they may, in fact, opt to aim higher in some areas. Cities should be empowered with the government's intervention powers.

Constitutional majorities

Government intervention in the case of failure – in public services for instance – should be a real option, but it should be considered only periodically and it should be the subject of a supermajority of two-thirds in parliament.

Funding

Cities should have the power to raise some of their own taxes, including business, property and sales based taxes, and to increase them, provided that an adequate proportion (perhaps 40–50%) of the electorate participate in the relevant mayoral election and that the property-related taxes borne by businesses and people are pegged such that they rise or fall together (so that non-voting businesses don't find themselves bearing a disproportionate share of the burden, as happened under the old rates system). Where funding and activity is devolved to cities this should be subject to appropriate fiscal transfers, including overheads for staff, and with the process subjected to independent scrutiny and adjudication (perhaps by the Office for Budget Responsibility). Local taxation powers would need to be balanced by the existing redistribution of tax revenues from rich and thriving areas to poorer, smaller ones via budget allocations.

Value for money, audit and scrutiny

If cities are to exercise functions that are currently those of departments accountable to parliament, then the National Audit Office should be involved in local audits and shold bring an annual report to parliament on the value for money of devolved cities. There would be a case for local Parliamentary Scrutiny Committees comprising MPs and others to strengthen oversight of city governance.

Applying these principles would involve a big adjustment by a political and policy class that is, in Britain, entirely unused to thinking with the patience, scale and long-term vision implied by these principles. This is as much a challenge to the cities as it is to government.

Above all, though, implementation of these principles needs to be accompanied by some significant policy changes. London's transformation to global city status was no accident: it was, at least in part, the result of very deliberate policy interventions, including large-scale and sustained transport investment and an industrial policy, of sorts, in the deregulation of financial services. As we saw in chapter 1, the market may have delivered London's transformation but state investment and intervention played a role too. Transport, industrial policy and innovation are all central. But the really important point when considering London isn't any particular scheme or institution but the sheer scale of investment, the patience with which successive governments have laid the foundations for the city's rise to greatness, and the vision of national, business and civic leaders. So, turning to look at the policy levers that are important for building our cities, it is worth reflecting on the most important thing of all. City building involves doing the right thing, at scale and for a very long time. The right policy ideas are at best a necessary, rather than a sufficient, part of the story, and they need to be accompanied by sustained commitment to the achievement of a bold long-term vision.

Geographical focus

I have deliberately been silent so far on what constitutes a city and I have blurred the boundaries between cities and urban areas. As soon as a city or urban area is defined, that becomes the focus of the debate. The economic and administrative footprints of most cities are very different. The new city regions that are forming now aren't perfect as economic regions, and urban areas exist in complex networks anyway. Economic life is both very local and yet global in scale. In the end, the boundaries don't matter that much, as long as there is adequate scale. The administrative footprint of Greater London is much smaller than that of the economy of the city. The same is true of Greater Manchester; the former because the government didn't follow through on the recommendations of the Herbert Commission and the latter because in 1972 Michel Heseltine's recommendations for the inclusion of North Cheshire in Greater Manchester were overturned by his own Conservative Party. Neither decision was economically rational but each city has still made progress, striking deals and making accommodations with its neighbours. Therefore, if we are to have a new agenda for cities, we should start with the geographies we have, according particular priority to some places, larger conurbations in the main, where policies for growth and inclusion could shift city and national performance.

The City Growth Commission[117] argued that fifteen major areas should be the focus: the former metropolitan counties in the main, plus London, Glasgow, Edinburgh, Belfast and the East Midlands. Along with the (generally larger) devolution deal areas, this list forms a sensible starting point for large-scale devolution. These are the areas in which one finds some of the greatest opportunity alongside a heavily disproportionate share of the people who need to be reconnected with the world of work. They are largely the areas developing the necessary political and administrative capacity to work across boundaries because they can see the benefits of doing so.

The agenda for cities that I set out below looks at all these issues in more detail and considers how policy might improve outcomes for cities, for the businesses based in them and for the people who live there. While devolution is far from a panacea, it is very hard to see how even the best city leaders could deliver change on the scale that is needed without stronger powers.

Making magnetic places

What makes cities attract like magnets? What makes people go and live in some places and stay there once they have arrived? Key on the list is a job, or, better still, the prospect of a career. Schools are also important. But other things matter too, particularly the ability to find housing of a kind that meets people's needs. This matters for everyone but it seems to be particularly important in places that are seeking to realign their economies in the hope of enticing from elsewhere the people they need to develop. This idea – that people choose attractive places to live – needs to be balanced against the other imperatives facing cities, not least the desire to reuse brownfield sites in and around urban centres. Aspiring working class and middle class people (and, more importantly, the financial, human and social capital they bring to the mix) can be persuaded to invest their capital in city centres, as we have seen in recent decades; regeneration areas are a much more difficult proposition unless there is scale and quality as well as amenity. 'Brownfield first' planning policies fail if they try to force people to buy homes in places they don't want to live, or perhaps more accurately if they don't reward would-be purchasers with an attractive enough offer in terms of both low cost and good local amenities, such as schools.

The cities of the North and the Midlands probably never had as much 'attractive' housing as southern ones, or as many communities that were rich in aspiring and affluent families. Restricting either the land supply to build out from successful parts of cities or failing to develop new sites serves to ensure that this doesn't change. The protection of greenfield and greenbelt sites is too often prioritized over everything else. Environmental degradation is a big issue for cities, but so too is the low-skills, low-pay equilibrium in which many places have become entrenched.[18] Restricting housing supply the way we do around cities now doesn't serve either set of concerns well, leading to sprawl and locking in urban poverty. Above all, though, it increases house prices. This isn't polemic: it is a reasonably well-researched fact. Our nation could scarcely have made a bigger mess of planning and housing policy in the last few decades.

Restricting the supply of housing increases houses prices significantly,[119] by at least 25% in the UK, while adding little to the much-needed densification of existing urban areas. Far from providing stability, restricting supply also increases price volatility.[120]

Transport matters

If agglomeration plays an important role in driving growth, then it is essential to create a critical mass and connectivity, with deep pools of available talent to fuel the growing sectors of the economy. Transport therefore has a pivotal role to play. There are also any number of social and environmental reasons why transport matters. It is vital, though, that the economic role of transport is viewed as being far more central than has historically been the case when transport investment decisions have been made. The right transport investment decisions drive agglomeration and economic inclusion: radiating the impact of city centres and other hot spots into their economic hinterlands, and in the process making growth in population and employment in these areas more likely in the long term than would be the case without connectivity. So intra-city connectivity matters: the investments that create links between the places where people live and where they work. The relative proximity of many British cities to each other and their relatively small size make it both possible and necessary for transport to play a role in growing 'travel-to-work flows' as well as cementing the functional economic linkages between cities. The implications of this for transport investment are clear: it should be high, overcoming decades of low investment that has resulted in slow and unreliable journeys. It should be focused on sustainable growth much more than on political priorities, and it should be designed and priced to encourage the broadest range of travellers, including traditional non-commuters, to use it. For whatever reason this is something that hasn't always featured in the pricing of recent light rapid transit systems. As to whether HS2, the Northern Powerhouse Rail network or road projects have priority, the message of everything we've looked at so far is clear: in the long run, these are not choices; they are all vitally important and need to form a phased programme. In this, if not in other respects, the evidence from Victorian Britain is as unambiguously clear as that from London more recently: we just need to get on with it.

The role and scope of industrial policy

In some policy areas it really isn't clear what constitutes the right thing to do. Nowhere is this truer than industrial policy. The policy cupboard looks very thinly stocked with interventions that work in the open, liberal economy we have, given our idiosyncratically low-skill, low-capital-intensity economy of two hundred years standing. Cities can and should be at the heart of redefining what industrial policy means because so much industry is located in specific cities.

Some commentators disagree. Janan Ganesh of the *Financial Times* expressed a view common among those comfortable with the plight of the giro towns of formerly industrial Britain described earlier:[121] 'The quiet success of Britain's anarchic economic model' is something we should be proud of, he argues, having moved beyond the rigidity of our more doctrinaire past and, in doing so, past our old rivals in France, and maybe even in Germany too, in creating a model that has fixed the generations-old British disease. Yet British productivity figures are dire. Only if London and the greater South East are taken in isolation does the picture look at all rosy. As chapter 1 described, the performance of most of our cities has been rather weak relative to the national average, with only tentative recent improvement.

For a decade or more after 1979, laissez faire policy prevailed, with the emphasis on information-based business support. Yet the government's own What Works Centre's review of business advice found little robust evidence to back up the notion that traditional business support adds long-term value:[122] signposting, business advice and mentoring may be things that a place should do to help promote business, but not if we expect them to make a major contribution to GVA. The same is probably true of large-scale government enterprise programmes, based on my experience evaluating them: usually highly targeted, focused on a market failure, so engineered against fraud and so thinly spread that they often fail by design.

The cry comes from protectionists and the left that we must protect national champions with financial support. Simple and large-scale subsidy is often proposed, as was the case early in 2016 to support the Port Talbot steelworks. Yet the evidence of most studies, including the Aston University study for the Manchester Independent Economic Review, suggests that subsidies don't work either, even in the medium term.[123] There is usually a jurisdiction offering a bigger subsidy somewhere in the world. Businesses can and do hop the globe in search of them. Enterprise Zones are a particular case in point, here, with most evaluations showing them to be poor value for money,[124] though US Empowerment Zones may be more effective.[125] This is not to argue there is nothing to be done though.

The starting point of our analysis of the Industrial Revolution was an analysis of the conditions precedent. Modern industrial policy should start from here too. I'm often amazed by how few cities, businesses or indeed their representative organizations have a really clear grasp of key basic concerns for business. Principal among these is often the availability of an adequate supply of sites and premises for business, large and small. Too often a designation on a map is confused with a real site or building for a business that needs it today, the difference between the two often being a year or two of investment and site preparation. It is hardly surprising then that many places lose investment to cities that are more ready for business. A good starting point, therefore, is to audit supply and demand for commercial office, distribution and industrial space and to debate with businesses about what's needed to sustain growing companies. In how many cities is this happening? Not enough, would be my guess.

One of the hoariest of old chestnuts in economic development (dating back to the so-called Macmillan gap in the 1930s[126]) is the availability or otherwise of capital: whether we have lower than optimal capital investment in companies and, if so, whether that is because there is an insufficiency of investable propositions or because inefficient debt and equity providers ration capital access (which would perhaps be unsurprising in an economy that has been in a low-demand, low-supply equilibrium for generations). The best guess is that all of this is happening: there are insufficient prime investable propositions in many cities, and many entrepreneurs may well be unrealistic. Secondly, at the same time, banks, particularly post Basel II, have been particularly cautious, expensive and, for too many entrepreneurs, out of reach, while equity investors used to flipping property assets in growing city property markets have often been unprepared to look seriously at portfolio-based venture capital investment in tech business. This very much fits with the path-dependent approach described in chapter 1, and even seems to be an issue in London's tech sector,[127] to which a third phenomenon might be added, in many cities: declinism.

Britain's retreat from Empire was a traumatic experience for all our industrial centres and ports. As deep as the decline of Manchester, Glasgow, Hull and Liverpool was, after a while it became so dominant as a narrative that it became the issue above all others. 'Declinism' set in.[128] This term is used to describe a type of political narrative that emerges in economies at certain times that attributes sometimes overly historical and sociological explanations to essentially economic phenomena. This can lead to views of historical inevitability rather than more benign views founded on a better reading of economic data that are inherently cyclical, or at least to a degree economically endogenous and subject to policy influence. As the literature on declinism makes clear, once this view takes hold it is both hard to shift and can become self-fulfilling. Getting the facts right and understanding what they mean is massively important. Manchester's experience and the use it made of the Independent Economic Review it undertook remains the case study for cities interested in making evidence work to support sound policy.[129]

OVERCOMING DECLINISM IN INDUSTRIAL POLICY: BRING BACK TEXTILES!

Greater Manchester has had some initial success in growing the textiles sector via the Alliance Project, which sought the repatriation of UK textiles manufacturing.[130] The project was undertaken jointly with one of the industry's most experienced leaders, Lord Alliance, formerly the chairman of N. Brown, with the support of ministers from the Department for Business, Innovation & Skills. It started with a very extensive and detailed research report that was used to inform everything that followed. This in turn helped secure government support for the initiative.

The project was semi-independent of the local authorities in the city and it was undertaken almost as a political project, led by a textiles expert and the former local MP Lorna Fitzsimons. This was vital because it helped to counter the prevailing sentiment in the city: that there was nothing that could be done to revive the sector. The emphasis was on starting to create positive momentum with the remaining textiles companies that had sustainable competitive models of growth and development. In doing this, Manchester has been able to tap into what is still a globally significant view of Manchester as a city of excellence in textiles and clothing, with 'made in Manchester' and 'made in England' still providing brand advantage in global markets.

This, together with strong marketing and good relationships with businesses and government, has started to create momentum, jobs and growth. Cotton spinning has returned to the city on a small scale for the first time in thirty years,[131] with both the Alliance Project and the Greater Manchester combined authority providing financial support through a combination of loans and grants to support the creation of 120 new jobs. If these initial projects turn out to be successful, there is no reason why, over the next period, the project and the combined authority should not take equity positions: providing cornerstone investment in new or existing innovative companies, building on the success of the local authority-owned Manchester Airport and other commercial ventures. This sort of initiative may work or it may not. The early signs are positive. But the notion that the government would have led the way is groundless, and neither were private investors queuing up. If we want experimentation in terms of both policy and the means to implement it, it is better left to the people for whom it matters most, and to the cities that are living with the legacy of past failure.

Picking winners: it can work but usually doesn't

The move of the BBC to what became Media City in Manchester isn't usually thought of as an exercise in picking winners, but that is what it was. This was a sector where the city was already strong, with a robust and growing base of companies. This was recognized and championed by the BBC Trust, resulting in the location of BBC (and later ITV) facilities at the Salford site and, as of the summer of 2016, its doubling with a further £1 billion of investment. Manchester had courted the BBC for years – something that was important when the BBC picked the city. The BBC itself is precisely the sort of anchor institution that cities undervalue at their peril. It is both high-value-added and internationally significant, not wholly in the private and traded sector of the economy, and of sufficient scale (as a potential customer or employer) to make a significant difference to the rest of the sector in the city. This gives it a public mission in which can be found the rationale for a decision that can – and, in the case of Media City, did – have transformative potential for both the place and the organization that chose it. So there was a rationale for Manchester to chase the BBC and for the BBC to do what, to some critics of the move, seemed irrational. The exception? Probably not, but it is not the rule either. As discussed above, picking winners too often means spending scarce resources delaying inevitable change instead of helping to prepare for it.

So places have a balance to strike – and nowhere more so than in relation to industrial policy – between aiming for the unattainable or doing too little. More often than not the data will tell you all you need to know. If rents for the best offices in town are £10 per square foot, unless there is an identified occupier or new transport development that might change matters, cities would be well advised to avoid picking a different kind of 'winner': supporting grade A offices that in most provincial cities need rents at two or three times that level if projects are to pay their way. It is better to invest in place shaping, transport, skills, public realm or other projects (the equivalents of the BBC and textiles projects described above) that should lead the place over time into a higher-value part of the market.

Innovation as industrial policy

There are exceptions to the rule of following the data. One example is when Manchester started to back a major expansion of support for incubation space for university-related technology businesses, to bring academia and the economy closer together. The city had earlier learnt (to its cost) in East Manchester that such investments are highly location sensitive, and that academics like to cluster near universities not in campuses on the other side of town. Later, it used its leverage with developers, putting the city up in lights at world property investment forums as a centre for science, inviting its development community and newcomers to adapt their offers to build more incubators for science-based businesses. The result was new private investment in the Manchester Science Park next to the University of Manchester. There was private sector support for the development of other labs too and eventually, when Astra Zeneca decided to pull out of its research campus south of the city, for the now-emboldened private sector to bid, successfully, to take over its running. The year before all this started, I recall a major firm of surveyors telling the city and one of its big technology firms that there was no market for labs in the city. There wasn't at that moment, as there was precious little supply, but there ought to have been because the conditions were there. It took the right balance of civic leadership, private capital and public support to change matters, and not the wild speculative punt that many city authorities are often invited to make. The result is a virtuous circle that saw, at around the same time, the city take the lead in persuading the government to back the Nobel Prize-winning team behind the discovery of graphene, first isolated in the city, resulting in the £70 million National Graphene Institute, and thereafter came investments by Abu Dhabi and China in the Graphene Enterprise and Innovation Centre and an important corporate spin-off.

Every city has examples of this nature. But what often lies behind them is strong institutions (in Manchester, my former organization New Economy played a key role in the process, working between the local authorities and the universities) and even stronger relationships. In Manchester, most change has involved brokering by Mr – or rather Sir – Manchester: Howard Bernstein. For every city thinking about innovation or enterprise, it is vital to both invest in the development of the city 'offer' and to think about how it is best advanced with the institutions and alliances needed to manage risk and deliver success, with its most empowered citizens being ready to roll their sleeves up and lead themselves.

No city has got innovation policy right yet. As we saw in chapter 1 it ought to be the lynchpin of industrial policy: the catalyst in industrial cities for the transition from old to new technologies, markets and forms of wealth creation. The goal must be the more systematic joining of the world-class academic endeavour of our universities with the enterprising businesses of our cities. This means working out how to get more graduates working in small and medium-sized firms. The expansion of Catapult centres arising from Hermann Hauser's review[132] is a good starting point for how cities wanting to institutionalize and improve their innovation might do so. City government should catalyse action where needed and invest where appropriate, but an innovation ecosystem needs businesses, large and small, to drive it and it needs institutions of business innovation to be created and sustained.

Human capital and development: the need for change

Arguably, Britain's two biggest domestic problems are the nation's low level of productivity and its high levels of inequality. These are not unrelated phenomena. On the contrary: they are a product of our history of development, and nowhere more so than in our cities and in the industries that gave birth to them. In the devolution process to date, there has been an emphasis on physical capital spending, and too little focus on the potential gains of improving the stock of human capital – spending on which happens to sit in the revenue account, largely out of scope, and in the 'too hard' box, so that little purposeful progress has been made. From early years, through school, in technical education and in welfare to work, we need to massively raise our game. So in addition to the reforms set out below, there is a strong case for local leadership on people issues in cities. The next round of devolution should include strong encouragement for the elected mayors to appoint high-profile education commissioners, with a degree of independence, taking on the role of the current regional schools commissioner and having responsibility for driving up performance.

In chapter 1 we saw how the British model of schooling almost certainly held back the development of industry in the nineteenth century, contributing to relative British economic decline. The fact that the role of colleges in vocational training is so hampered by poor outcomes from schooling is testament to the fact that we haven't fixed the system yet. Worse than that, the stability that places need from their schools has been undermined by decades of micromanagement from well-meaning ministers and councils alike, creating and abolishing institutions with alacrity. Schools should be the strongest pillars of every place: well-known, loved and valued institutions, supported by government, business and communities; a vital part of the patrimony of place. Many are anything but that: renamed, reorganized and the subject of little more than political whim (such as recent moves to recreate grammar schools). What goes on inside schools in many cities matters much more yet remains inadequate, with one in three schools (many of them urban) in the North and Midlands requiring improvement.[133]

Academic education, while imperfect, does function as a means of preparing young people for university. Our system of technical education, such as it is, does not succeed in creating a pathway with anything like the same level of success for young people taking a vocational route into employment. It is a very old problem too. The proposal for grammar, technical and secondary modern schools with parity of esteem in the 1944 Education Act was never achieved, either in principle or in practice. Attempts since then through City Technology Colleges and Vocational Diplomas, and more recently through University Technical Colleges, have all nibbled away at an issue that will need a more purposeful approach in our cities if growing parts of our urban economies are going to be able to hire people with the skills and aptitudes they need.[134]

The need to invest further in people was central to the recommendations of the Manchester Independent Economic Review. Its first priority, and one borne out subsequently by the work of the Early Intervention Review, is that early years – the period between conception and school, in which a child's life chances are significantly formed – is vital but remains a relatively neglected area of policy.[135] Research in the US has found a gap of 30 million words between what kids on welfare and the richest hear by the age of three. If, as follow-up studies have found, this has a lasting impact on life chances, then the ad hoc, voluntary and altogether inadequate arrangements we currently have look wholly inadequate, placing too much burden on parents for what is a major societal issue.[136] The pay-off may take a generation to feed through to the urban economy, but its importance could not be greater to city success.

The links between skills and industrial policy

One of the key findings of the Alliance Project was the existence of a shortage of machinists for the clothing sector. This example is one among many reasons why

Manchester and other places have sought devolution of skills spending. There has been no more contested space in devolution policy than skills over recent years, with partial delegation of strategic responsibility secured (and then rescinded) and partial devolution occurring in the last couple of years. Even then, this was only in respect of already significantly reduced adult skills budgets and with joint liability with government for instituting reform of local skills systems. This, despite the fact that colleges are much more dependent on the funding for 16–19 year olds, which is still the sole responsibility of government. Cities have been invited to participate in distributing what is, in effect, the government's painful restructuring medicine. Nor has the government shown any willingness to devolve responsibility for apprenticeships, leaving the levers to influence policy detached from urban labour markets.

If the British skills system worked well, perhaps the case for the government's rather dogmatic stance against devolution would be justified. But it doesn't, and it isn't. Not by a long way. Colleges argue, rightly, that they spend too much of their urban budgets on remedial activity because they have to help too many functionally illiterate and innumerate young people from city schools. But this has been the case for the last twenty years, to my certain knowledge, and probably for years before that too. Nothing much has changed, not even the fact that FE tends to take the brunt of funding cuts.[137]

Although colleges train people for vital trades in sectors such as construction, the evidence tends to suggest that their efforts – and, more importantly, the efforts of the young people themselves – are to a degree wasted because employers often don't value the qualifications they offer. Employers continue to be more concerned with skills gained on the job than with college-based qualifications (another echo of nineteenth-century attitudes). Meanwhile, higher-level apprenticeships have gone unfilled for years, for want of enough young people with the GCSEs needed to enter them. None of these problems, or a host of other issues, is new. The system doesn't work for learners, for colleges, for the communities they serve or, in the end, for the country.

Every attempt to secure strong devolution has been met with resistance from government departments whose commitment to system stability and a national model, even if it is a not very good one, seems to be of paramount importance to them. Here is an area where devolutionary experimentation ought to be more purposefully pursued: not to replace a college-/provider-driven system of the kind we have now, but to put employers in a more central role in driving the system. The employer voice in this too often goes unheard. This is as much an issue for employers as for anyone, with businesses often expressing different needs in surveys than they do in their training and hiring plans: saying they want high skills but in fact competing through lower pay and qualifications and on-the-job training. So the priority should be on putting skills in the hands of employers, but with public funds used to leverage change more than to subsidize regular training, stewarding the skills of people on an institutionally strong and ongoing basis. This latter point is important. If the goal is to move our cities into higher-skilled labour market equilibria, it is vital that leadership of local skills means precisely that: brokering the creation in key areas of the economy of skills escalators, perhaps using the new training levy on a localized basis as a lever in local supply chains.

The performance of the skills system is so poor and longstanding that it is hard to see how the proposal here could be worse than the status quo. In summer 2016 yet another report was produced on this issue: the Sainsbury Review, which the government has taken forward via its Skills Plan. There are grounds for believing that this may enable us to make progress.[138] But as matters stand, there is no meaningful institutional mechanism to enable local areas to shape the local skills system, and there certainly needs to be or the approach will be destined to fail. This is another area where local innovation could make a big difference.

The human cost of change: people, place and adjustment

There is a plausible argument that the cities of Britain are making a comeback but we are a long way away from a position where enough of the communities in Britain where the economic tide went out forty years ago and hasn't come back in since are being helped. As discussed earlier in the context of the EU referendum, working out how to create momentum in such areas is now a national priority. One legacy of post-war corporatism and a far from wholly successful period of liberal reform is an essentially broken contract between many British people and the state. The generations before mine grew up with a deal: if you're a good pupil, pass your exams, work hard, be socially responsible, etc., our economy and society will reward you and your family. For too many, a decent home, a career and the absence of financial fear are a distant dream. If this is the case, for too many people, and for too long, the political expression of citizenship our country asks people to express at the ballot box isn't really backed up by an adequate or fully shared enough economic citizenship. Viewed in this way, the fracturing of our politics makes more sense.

Supply-side policies have a role to play in changing matters. Active labour market policy provides a strong stimulus to people to get on the best rung of the labour market ladder that they can, and ensures that those who could but choose not to do so are sanctioned. But what about the hundreds of thousands of people in the country for whom active policy, multiple interventions, a powerfully growing labour market and massive public sector intervention in the period up to 2008 did not deliver jobs? Their communities felt like they were stuck in a post-industrial rut. Even instinctive supply siders would have to pause and wonder whether this isn't in the nature of a demand-side problem. Thirty years of highly aggressive supply-side policy seems to have had a limited impact after all.

For too many people, conditional benefits have been interspersed with poor work experience. They have tried and failed, again and again, either on the Work Programme or on a myriad of previous schemes. They are therefore left to an unconditional regime that recognizes that they have no real likelihood of getting work in the hard world of the regular labour market. In our towns and cities there are hundreds of thousands of people in this situation. Some cannot work. Some could perform certain work. But they are not scroungers. In ways that people who live in the hard-bitten areas of our country understand quite well, not working later in life became a mass habit that has lasted too long for regular incentives to work. Arguably, the problem with large parts of industrial urban Britain is that they have lost their *raison d'être* in such a profound way that some of what might be thought of as normal market mechanisms aren't working. Or, if they are, their effect in many communities is producing undesirable consequences, concentrating long-term unemployment and exclusion. Those who can do so, get out. Aspirations fall in many communities. Expectations fall further. Mental health problems soar, along with family breakdown and alcohol and substance abuse, the social and financial costs of which are now unaffordably high.

The frequent result of this in certain areas of many cities is a residualizing effect, as those who can leave do so, leaving a concentration of lower-income communities often characterized by three dominant groups: the traditional white working class; minority, often South Asian, communities; and newly arriving migrants. Those in the former two categories owe their presence in the area to the usually now-departed former staple industry. It is these communities that were often ill prepared for the permanent changes affecting them. While many found work or moved or both, in many areas a sizeable number remained and many are not in employment, even when employment is theoretically available in what most would consider a reasonable travel-to-work area.[139] This is the root of the issue. Neither a benevolent-but-undemanding state nor punitive sanctions alone are the way forward in delivering improved jobs and social mobility. And nor is a purely centrally led approach. Evidence on what drives and impedes intergenerational mobility doesn't really exist. The evidence that geography matters is strong. There are, in all probability, 'unlearnt lessons' in our cities – lessons that our new metro mayors will need to understand.[140]

Even when the state was investing heavily, traditional policy has tended not to work for a variety of reasons, principal among which is the siloed nature of government policy described earlier. It fails to break what might be called a triple lock on communities, where there is something of a localized labour demand deficit. These are places where economic activity rates are low and where, firstly, policy that just aims to help individuals (the basis of welfare for decades now), when it is successful, leads them to exit the area, with out-movers, if they are replaced at all, often replaced by poorer incomers. Secondly, policy to improve the physical infrastructure of deprived areas (housing enveloping schemes) seems not to have produced a change in the trajectory of many communities in an economic sense: it doesn't generate jobs and it doesn't give places enough sense of hope either. These policies and the 'housing plus' initiatives of social housing providers prove to be too small scale to counter the forces of economic change and countervailing national policy. Thirdly, low labour market attachment and weak skills ensure that the resident population remains poorly placed to access employment, fuelling both alienation among many who stay and mobility among those who can choose.

This triple lock has proved almost impossible to break. If there are three aspects to the problem – economic (demand), personal (supply) and physical – then the solution must either tackle all three together or it must approach them in a coordinated way. Policies aimed at only one, and possibly those aimed at two, don't work.

They can actually make matters worse. If people and place both matter (a hugely controversial area among economists, who fail to grasp the reality that both are important), a different approach is needed. The issue of labour demand needs to be addressed. The root problem is long-term unemployment and labour market disconnection. The goal is simple: to create momentum in every community that the place is improving, and that there is hope beyond a choice between benefits, on the one hand, and poorly paid and unstable employment with little or no hope of progression on the other.

Welfare revisited

The market will take care of some of this if a concerted effort is made by cities' business and civic leaders. Infra-structure spending could make a big difference, as the cost to government has literally never been cheaper. But more will be needed, not least the development of links that bind the different elements of government intervention together to create momentum. National policy needs to regulate the 'gig economy' by raising the floor of the labour market nationally, but there needs to be a local element too. At its heart, the approach would need to have a locally driven, temporary, 'community jobs' element – paid at modest wages with training, and with a focus on older people, targeting those less likely to get work anyway – to reduce the cost of what can be an expensive approach. These 'intermediate labour market programmes' have been proven to be effective. The much-derided Future Jobs Fund sought to reduce youth unemployment through paid temporary work placements at the end of the last Labour government's period in office. It delivered benefit, measured in the thousands of pounds per participant, to young people on the programme, to employers, to society and even to the exchequer.[141]

Some advocates of supply-side policy would no doubt find the return of temporary employment programmes abhorrent, bringing to mind a memory of the Manpower Services Commission in the 1970s. They aren't a panacea, certainly, but those same critics have to answer a question that they have failed to answer in all the years of supply-side driven reform: how can we get more of the 20–30% of people in our cities who have not had fulfilling working lives since the traditional industries declined (or indeed more of their descendants, many of whom haven't had fulfilling working lives either) back into work that offers dignity to them and their communities and labour to our economy? The Future Jobs Fund that was run by local government worked (though better in some areas than others, admittedly). Most, if not all, of the more traditional welfare-to-work programmes end up sending three-quarters of the people who go on them, or even more, back to the benefits regime from which they came. The message to them and their families is that they have failed, again. This strikes me as making people endure what Jonathan Wolff describes as 'avoidable humiliation', the very source of the low-aspiration, low-expectation culture that blights many urban areas.[142] We will not fix our cities until we do better for the people who live in them.

Democracy and the commons

Grass roots democracy is fundamental to making local government work, and this is certainly the case with the new mayoralties. There are people who argue that the city region mayoralties are undemocratic. I disagree and I don't think any apology is needed for the way we got to this point. The brute power of the national state that was used to take power away from our cities has been used to start giving it back. It is now down to the cities themselves to use that power, and that process should start with engaging people with the powers being devolved, taking views on how they are used, and listening to what people want. It doesn't mean referenda. I would rather we stuck with our tradition of representative democracy and persuaded voters that power and sovereignty are being returned to them through devolution. Rather than criticize the so-called elites who negotiated the deals (the elected members and their officers), we would do better, as Tristram Hunt recently argued,[143] to encourage people to elect mayors that have the skills and aptitude needed to run great cities. So a good start to rebuilding the civic could be made with wide engagement in the selection of candidates, a healthy pre-election debate and campaigns designed to maximize turnout rather than the core-voter strategies that have been the norm in much local and national campaigning.

Where the critics are onto something, even if their aim is wrongly directed, is picked up by Simon Parker in his exploration of the notion of the commons: the unowned and unownable elements of every place.[144] Drawing on a range of economic and social litera-ture, Parker, among others, makes the argument for a far richer debate on the role of the common good in society and the development of local places. This is a timely reminder that recent attempts to do this nationally, either through social capital under the last Labour government or via the 'Big Society' under the coalition, both ran into the sand. In the case of the for-mer, the now-abolished 'baby bonds' would have made significant inroads into communities, and some of the smaller initiatives seeded under the latter may yet too. But it seems perverse that so much social capital and community building should need to be encouraged by the central state. All the more so if the key priority is anchoring local places and the people who live there with powerful local institutions.

Even if they trade and provide quasi-government services, social enterprises can offer a local counterpoint to the powerful and often remote forces that shape local communities. There seems to be more mileage in this route than more traditional ideas. Local exchange and trading schemes have rarely been shown to work beyond essentially well-heeled communities. Credit unions, as important as they are, do not seem to have displaced either the moneylender or the tyranny of high-street retailers offering credit on terms nearly as onerous. But we are building from a low base. In one of my last projects in Manchester, the aim of which was to stimulate the creation of more social enterprises, our research found that, once a small number of large charities were stripped out, the social enterprise sector as a player in the economy or in public services was virtually non-existent, with median annual turnover of £175,000.[145] The same is not true in other British cities, notably Glasgow and Birmingham, both of which have more vibrant social economy sectors.

Empowered citizens are a vital part of successful communities. The third sector has a key role to play in this process of empowerment, and social enterprises are an important way of delivering the power of financial capital and institutional wealth to poorer communities.

Getting people into work, making communities feel that they have hope, and investing in education and skills – breaking the triple lock described earlier – must be the starting point, but the lesson from the history of British cities and of working people more generally, as told in Jonathan Rose's account of the same, is that people and communities organizing is vital if they are to lock in the benefits of growth and prosperity and of enabling working people to participate in the intellectual life of cities in a way they don't generally do today.[146] In practice, this means cities choosing to run public services in a way that allows social enterprises to bid for them successfully, at and beyond the levels required by the Social Value Act, and encouraging entrepreneurs to set up social businesses, providing capital and support, enriching the institutional fabric of communities. It should also mean cities proactively supporting arts organizations, not just for the intrinsic value they provide, but because the evidence, even if tentative, mounts that organizations in areas as diverse as heritage[147] and music[148] have a significant institutional and instrumental value to add to the communities they serve.[149]

If the central argument of this book is that big national government doesn't hold all the answers, it is important to be clear that powerful city government doesn't either unless it is embedded in, and fully part of, the life of the community it serves.

Afterword

My main questions here concerned whether British cities in the 2020s could match the achievements of Victorian cities and, if so, how. I have made the case that while they made Britain a very rich place in some important respects, the cities – and none more so than Manchester – created a mould for our urban industrial culture that has not served us well compared with our international competitors. Chapter 1 established that the cities created wealth but not an enduringly successful economic and social model.

Chapter 2 found that the roots of long-term decline could also be traced back to the social and cultural model of the nineteenth-century cities. In social care and public health, perhaps the better models came later: from Joseph Chamberlain's Birmingham, whose *grand projets* were emulated by every city in late Victorian Britain. In this respect, Manchester's current approach, with the public authorities leading the charge for regeneration and renewal, actually has a rather Brummie lilt to it. But the scale of Victorian ambition has yet to be fully seen, let alone delivered or surpassed, anywhere.

Religious freedom played an important role in the story told here. Today, organized religion plays a limited role in the life of our cities and virtually no role at all in the bonding social capital of their leaders. Yet religion has played a key role historically, not just in past achievements but in the values and some of the institutions that still form an important part of the economic and social life of cities. Yet there is no counterpart to this role in British industrial culture.

At various points in this story, reference has been made to the newness of British cities and the absence of a tradition of craft guilds or the statutory chambers and other more socialized forms of organization found in some other countries. This raises the question of whether we might have had a better experience of industrialization – stronger institutions, more enduring companies and a better system of innovation and skill formation – had our industrial culture had the same journey in industrial organization as was the case elsewhere. With roots in the guild tradition and other institutions and bonds formed but liberated by a century or two of more modern capitalist competition, we may have secured the best of both worlds – something that may be part of the success of both German cities and their industries.

The history of our cities cannot be rewritten. But there are lessons to learn and put into practice as we look to the future. Cities have moments to strike deals with their national states. One such moment was missed in the middle of the nineteenth century; another may beckon now as the economic power of cities is growing once again. In every aspect of investment in human life, from under-fives through school and education, not least further education, the cities of today and tomorrow need to do better than those of yesterday. But the cities can only afford to do better if they are better at innovation: turning ideas into jobs and wealth. This is likely to require a more investment-intensive economy than has been the norm for a generation, if ever. These are well-known challenges. If, as we go about rebuilding our cities, there is one less obvious lesson that shouts loudly from the foregoing, and which needs to underpin all our efforts to make progress, it is that we ought to take far closer interest in institutional design: in the powers of cities themselves and in the urban institutional legacy with which they and we equip future generations.

This is the moment to push forward with a new settlement for the UK's cities. The lessons from the Brexit vote, which took place as I was writing, are that the centralized UK economy and state have not served large portions of the population at all well. And the potential shock of leaving the EU to the sectors that have powered London's remarkable growth mean it is essential to enable other cities and other strengths to develop in the years ahead.

Endnotes

1. J. McDermott. 2015. Manchester: UK's new order? *Financial Times*, 20 February (http://on.ft.com/2iDyEyN).

2. D. Thomson. 1981. *England in the Twentieth Century*, p. 23. London: Pelican.

3. Devolution from the UK to Scotland, Wales and Northern Ireland may well have made inroads into this issue in those places.

4. P. M. Hohenberg. 2004. The historical geography of European cities: an interpretive essay. In *Handbook of Regional and Urban Economics*, chapter 67, volume 4, pp. 3021–3052. Elsevier.

5. P. Ackroyd. 2011. *The History of England*, volume 1, p. 411. London: Macmillan.

6. T. Hunt. 2004. *Building Jerusalem*, p. 4. London: Phoenix.

7. E. Evans. 2001. *The Forging of the Modern State*, p. 130. New York: Longman.

8. N. Crafts. 1985. *British Growth During the Industrial Revolution*. Oxford: Clarendon.

9. See J. Mokyr. 2009. *The Enlightened Economy*. Penguin. J. Mokyr. 2016. *A Culture of Growth: the Origins of the Modern Economy*. Princeton University Press. See also R. C. Allen. 2009. *The British Industrial Revolution in Global Perspective*. Cambridge University Press.

10. Mokyr (2009, chapter 2).

11. This has been a particularly contested area, especially post Nick Crafts's work (see Crafts (1985) and Mokyr (2009) as well as R. C. Allen. 2006. The British Industrial Revolution in global perspective: how commerce created the Industrial Revolution and modern economic growth. Preprint (http://bit.ly/2iDA6RM).

12. Evans (2001, p. 133).

13. Allen (2006).

14. Allen (2006).

15. See, for example, R. C. Allen. 2005. Capital accumulation, technological change, and the distribution of income during the British Industrial Revolution. Working Paper (http://bit.ly/2iDEoZr).

16. Evans (2001, p. 134).

17. See, for example, Crafts (1985) and Mokyr (2009).

18. Evans (2001, p. 136).

19. P. Hall. 1998. *Cities in Civilisation*, p. 315. London: Weidenfield & Nicholson.

20. Crafts (1985, p. 7).

21. Hall (1998, p. 318).

22. Hall (1998, p. 315).

23. N. Crafts. 2002. Productivity growth in the Industrial Revolution: a new growth accounting perspective. Working Paper (http://bit.ly/2hSyHrz).

24. N. Crafts. 1987. The industrial revolution: economic growth in Britain 1700–1860. *Recent Findings of Research in Economic & Social History*, Spring, Issue 4 .

25. A. Travis. 2011. Thatcher government toyed with evacuating Liverpool after 1981 riots. *The Guardian*, 30 December (http://bit.ly/2hSDPMA).

26. S. Parker. 2015. *Taking Back Power*, pp. 27–28. Bristol: Policy Press.

27. J. Jacobs. 2000. *The Death and Life of Great American Cities*, p. 304. New York: Pimlico.

28. E. Glaeser. 2011. *Triumph of the City: How Our Greatest Invention Makes Us Richer, Smarter, Greener, Healthier, and Happier*, p. 7. London: Penguin.

29. For an overview of the issue see J. Jefferies. 2005. The UK population: past, present and future. Office for National Statistics (http://bit.ly/2jhUk1Z).

30. As quoted on p. 7 of W. Ashworth. 1960. *An Economic History of England*. London: Methuen.

31. Ashworth (1960, p. 20).

32. L. Woessmann, S. O. Becker and E. Hornung. 2010. Being the educational world leader helped Prussia catch up in the Industrial Revolution. VoxEU blog, 9 May (http://bit.ly/2iDOVUp).

33. M. Roser and M. Nagdy. 2016. Primary education. Published online at OurWorldInData.org (http://bit.ly/2iDTZYO).

34. Crafts (1985, p. 159).

35. F. C. Montague. 1887. *Technical Education: A Summary of the Report of the Royal Commission Appointed to Inquire into the State of Technical Instruction*, p. 66. London: Cassell & Co. (http://bit.ly/2iDTyxx).

36. Montague (1887, p. 54).

37. Crafts (1985, p. 163).

38. A. Guagnini. 1993. Worlds apart: academic instruction and professional qualification in the training of mechanical engineers 1850–1914. In *Education and Industrial Performance in Europe, 1850 to 1939* (ed. R. Fox and A. Guagnini). Cambridge University Press.

39. Ashworth (1960, p. 244).

40. N. Crafts. 1996. Financing industry in the nineteenth century. *Recent Findings of Research in Economic & Social History*, Spring, Issue 22.

41. Crafts (1985, p. 157).

42. Ashworth (1960, p. 246).

43. H. J. Habakkuk. 1962. *American and British Technology in the Nineteenth Century: the Search for Labour-Saving Inventions*. Cambridge University Press. (Quoted in N. Crafts and K. H. O'Rourke. 2013. Twentieth century growth. Discussion Papers in Economic and Social History, no. 117, September (http://bit.ly/2hSHGJm).)

44. Barlow Report. 1940. *Royal Commission on the Distribution of the Industrial Population*, cmd 6153, chapter 2. London: HMSO.

45. Hall (1998, p. 309).

46. A. G. Haldane. 2015. Growing, fast and slow. Speech on behalf of the Bank of England given at the University of East Anglia, 17 February (http://bit.ly/2hSQpvi).

47. R. J. Gordon. 2016. Goodbye, golden age of growth. Bloomberg-View blog, 26 January (http://bloom.bg/2iDWs5u).

48. J. Simmie, J. Carpenter, A. Chadwick and R. Martin. 2008. *History Matters: Path Dependence and Innovation in British City-Regions*. NESTA Research Report, July, p. 20 (http://bit. ly/2iDSNo8).

49. Haldane (2015).

50. R. Lupton and A. Power. 2004a. The growth and decline of cities and regions. Report, London School of Economics and Political Science (http://bit.ly/2iCP4qY).

51. P. Cheshire, M. Nathan and H. Overman. 2014. *Urban Economics and Urban Policy*, p, 12. Worcester: Edward Elgar.

52. R. Lupton and A. Power. 2004b. The growth and decline of cities and regions. CASE Brookings Census Briefs, no. 1, July (http://bit.ly/ 2hSMSgk).

53. R. Martin, B. Gardiner and P. Tyler. 2014. The evolving economic performance of UK cities: city growth patterns 1981–2011. Working Paper, p. 13. Foresight, Government Office for Science (http://bit.ly/ 2hhEkgg).

54. My analysis data from P. Swinney and E. Thomas. 2015. A century of cities: urban economic change since 1911. Report, March, Centre for Cities, London (http://bit.ly/2hhzeR8).

55. Simmie *et al.* (2008).

56. Hohenberg (2004).

57. D. Dorling. 2014. The London problem: has the capital become too dominant? *New Statesman*, 4 September (http://bit.ly/2iE45bW).

58. HM Govt. 2012. http://bit.ly/2hhEkgg.

59. L. McGough and G. Piazza. 2016. 10 years of tax: how cities contributed to the national exchequer from 2004/05 to 2014/15. Report, July, Centre for Cities, London (http://bit.ly/2hSX88x).

60. For a discussion of US urban failure see A. Mallach (ed.). 2012. *Rebuilding America's Legacy Cities: New Directions for the Industrial Heartland*. The American Assembly.

61. This section is based heavily on M. Emmerich, J. Holden and R. Rios. 2012. Urban growth in the UK: a Mancunian call to action. Working Paper, New Economy.

62. See, for example, A. Harding, S. Marvin and B. Robson. 2006. A framework for city-regions. Report, February, Office of the Deputy Prime Minister (http://bit.ly/2hSURKk).

63. See, for example, Glaeser (2011). For a full discussion of the debate see R. Martin, B. Gardiner and P. Tyler. 2010. Does spatial agglomeration increase national growth? Some evidence from Europe. *Journal of Economic Geography* 11(6): 1–28.

64. See P. Kline and E. Moretti. 2013. Local economic development, agglomeration economies and the big push: 100 years of evidence from the Tennessee Valley Authority. Working Paper (http://bit.ly/2hT2UXH).

65. See What Works Centre for Local Economic Growth. 2015a. Evidence review 6: broadband. Report, March (http://bit.ly/2hT6aCl). What Works Centre for Local Economic Growth. 2015b. Evidence review 7: transport. Report, July (http://bit.ly/2hTdVlf) .

66. C. Haynes and V. Langley. 2014. Magnet cities. Report, KPMG (http://bit.ly/2hT4uJa).

67. For a summary see D. Gardner. 2016. The Evergreen Fund. Presentation, FI-Compass (http://bit.ly/2hTfbLt).

68. See, for example, 'Key features of common law or civil law systems' on the PPPIRC website (http://bit.ly/2iEbTdM).

69. Evans (2001, p. 141).

70. Quoted in Hunt (2004, p. 200).

71. B. Disraeli. 1844. *Conningsby*, volume II, book IV, chapter 1.

72. A. Briggs. 1963. *Victorian Cities*, p. 68. Pelican.

73. Evans (2001, p. 147).

74. See, for example, R. D. Putnam. 2001. *Bowling Alone: The Collapse and Revival of American Community*. New York: Simon & Schuster.

75. Evans (2001, p. 139).

76. B. Williams. 1985. *The Making of Manchester Jewry 1740–1875.* Manchester University Press.

77. Briggs (1963, p. 47).

78. D. Russell. 2004. *Looking North: Northern England and the National Imagination.* Manchester University Press.

79. N. Johnston. 2013. The history of the parliamentary franchise. House of Commons Library Research Paper 13/14, 1 March (http://bit.ly/2j5d1Gz).

80. Evans (2001, p. 196).

81. Hunt (2004, p. 287).

82. Briggs (1963, p. 20).

83. Hunt (2004, p. 311).

84. For an interesting comparative discussion on this and New Labour see S. Szreter. 2002. A central role for local government? The example of late Victorian Britain. Policy Paper, 2 May, History and Policy (http://bit.ly/2hT7GEg).

85. J. Wolff and C. Arscott. 1990. Cultivated capital: patronage and art in nineteenth-century Manchester and Leeds. In *Victorian Values: Personalities and Perspectives in Nineteenth Century Society* (ed. G. Marsden), p. 38. New York: Longman.

86. A. Effland. 1990. *A History of Art Education: Intellectual and Social Currents in Teaching the Visual Arts*, p. 57. New York: Teachers College Press.

87. Russell (2004, p. 208).

88. J. W. Pegg. 2003. Newcastle's musical heritage: an introduction (http://bit.ly/2hT21hy).

89. See J. Rose. 2001. *The Intellectual Life of the British Working Classes*, chapter 6. Yale University Press.

90. S. Gunn. 2000. *The Public Culture of the Victorian Middle Class*, p. 138. Manchester University Press.

91. See Rose (2001, pp. 455–464) for a discussion of modernism.

92. J. Major. 1993. Speech to the Conservative Group for Europe on 22 April (http://bit.ly/2hTeT7x).

93. L. Mackay. 2011. UKUKUKUKUK. *London Review of Books*, 30 August.

94. Glaeser (2011, p. 13).

95. Quoted in Briggs (1963, p. 72).

96. The Reverend James Shergold Boone (1844), quoted in Hunt (2004, p. 46).

97. Quoted in M. Weiner. 1981. *English Culture and the Decline of the Industrial Spirit 1850–1980*, p. 88. London: Penguin.

98. Weiner (1981, p. 13).

99. Quoted in Briggs (1963, p. 72).

100. Weiner (1981, p. 14).

101. Quoted in Parker (2015, p. 93).

102. P. Shore. 1977. Inner cities (government proposals). Hansard, HC Deb, 6 April, volume 929, cc1226-46 (http://bit.ly/2hT5ZqE). See also Emmerich *et al.* (2012) for a discussion of anti-urban policy bias.

103. P. Hennessy (1989). *Whitehall*, p. 707. London: Secker & Warburg.

104. Giro here has two significances, describing both the means by which unemployment benefits were paid and a cultural reference point of the time because of mass unemployment. See S. Townsend. 2014. Sue Townsend: how the welfare state left me and my kids scouring the streets for pennies. *The Guardian*, 13 April (http://bit.ly/2iEencs).

105. For a discussion see C. Hood. 2001. New public management. In *International Encyclopedia of the Social & Behavioral Sciences*. Elsevier (http://bit.ly/2iEkCwx).

106. See, for example, R. Blaug, L. Horner and R. Lekhi. 2006. Public value, politics and public management: a literature review. Project Report, Work Foundation, London.

107. The Marmot Review. 2010. *Fair Society, Healthy Lives*, p. 11. UCL Institute of Health Equity (http://bit.ly/2j59fga).

108. MIER was a major review undertaken in Manchester. See http://manchester-review.co.uk, and note 129 below.

109. G. Russell, P. Stowe, J. Twomey and B. Robson. 2009. Sustainable communities. *Manchester Independent Economic Review* (http://bit.ly/2hUcET8).

110. MORI poll (http://bit.ly/2kvMjrg) quoted in Parker (2015, p. 22).

111. Glaeser (2011, p. 101).

112. F. Fukayama. 2005. *State Building Governance and World Order in the Twenty-First Century*, pp. 94–96. London: Profile Books.

113. R. Caro. 1974. *The Power Broker: Robert Moses and the Fall of New York*. Knopf.

114. See S. Jenkins. 2015. The secret negotiations to restore Manchester to greatness. *The Guardian*, 12 February (http://bit.ly/2hU6VwF).

115. B. Katz and J. Bradley. 2013. *The Metropolitan Revolution: How Cities and Metros Are Fixing Our Broken Politics and Fragile Economy*. Brooking Institution Press. B. R. Barbour. 2013. *If Mayors Ruled the World: Dysfunctional Nations, Rising Cities*. Yale University Press.

116. See, for example, OECD. 2015. Local economic leadership. LEED Programme Report (http://bit.ly/2hU8YAx).

117. RSA and City Growth Commission. 2014. Unleashing metro growth: final recommendations of the city growth commission. Report, October (http://bit.ly/2hU2CS2).

118. See David Soskice and David Finegold's seminal paper on Britain's training problem: D. Soskice and D. Finegold. 1988. The failure of training in Britain: analysis and prescription. *Oxford Review of Economic Policy* 4(3): 21–53.

119. Cheshire *et al.* (2014, pp. 100–101) has a good summary of the evidence.

120. Cheshire *et al.* (2014, p. 88).

121. J. Ganesh. 2016. The quiet success of Britain's anarchic economic model. *Financial Times*, 4 April (http://on.ft.com/2iST6vi).

122. See the What Works Centre for Local Economic Growth business advice summary at http://bit.ly/2iT2vTA/.

123. N. Driffield and J. Love. 2009. Inward and indigenous investment. *Manchester Independent Economic Review* (http://bit.ly/2iSW9TV).

124. See Cheshire *et al.* (2014, p. 38).

125. What Works Centre for Local Economic Growth. 2015a. Evidence review 10: area based initiatives. Report, January (see the executive summary at http://bit.ly/2hU8niE).

126. For a discussion see P. Scott and L. Newton. 2006. Jealous monopolists? British banks and responses to the Macmillan Gap during the 1930s. Working Paper 2006-036, Henley Business School, University of Reading (http://bit.ly/2hUTrQZ).

127. See p. 2293 of M. Nathan and E. Vandore. 2014. Here be startups: exploring a young digital cluster in inner East London. *Environment and Planning A* 46(10): 2283–2299.

128. See, for example, J. Tomlinson. 2009. Thrice denied: 'declinism' as a recurrent theme in British history in the long twentieth century. *Twentieth Century British History* 20(2): 227–251.

129. See the What Works Centre for Local Economic Growth 'Using evidence: Greater Manchester case study' blog and resources at http://bit.ly/2hUfqHO.

130. Alliance Project Team. 2015. Repatriation of UK textiles manufacture. Report for The Greater Manchester Combined Authority, January (http://bit.ly/2iSYpe6).

131. A. Bounds. 2016. Restored cotton mill to drive rebirth of textiles industry. *Financial Times*, 7 August (http://on.ft.com/2iTooyY).

132. H. Hauser. 2014. Review of the Catapult network: recommendations on the future shape, scope and ambition of the programme. Report BIS/14/1085 (http://bit.ly/2iSZjr0).

133. M. Willshaw. 2016. Speech at 'Transforming cities, the case for education and transport', Institute for Public Policy Research seminar, 23 February (http://bit.ly/2iSZWkm).

134. For a discussion on this see J. West and H. Steedman. 2003. Finding our way: vocational education in England. Report, Centre for Economic Performance, London School of Economics and Political Science (http://bit.ly/2iTe9ov).

135. See G. Allen. 2011. Early intervention: smart investment, massive savings – the second independent report to Her Majesty's Government (http://bit.ly/2iT2YoB).

136. For a summary of the work on 'The Thirty Million Word Gap' by University of Kansas researchers Betty Hart and Todd R. Risley, visit http://bit.ly/2iT8SpQ.

137. For a comparative international analysis see M. Kuczera, S. Field and H. C. Windisch. 2016. Building skills for all: a review of England – policy insights from the survey of adult skills. OECD Skills Studies Report (http://bit.ly/2iToMot).

138. Department for Education, Department for Business, Innovation & Skills and N. Boles. 2016. Post-16 skills plan and independent report on technical education. Policy Paper (http://bit.ly/2iT5wTK).

139. For an example in London see London Borough of Barking and Dagenham. 2016. No-one left behind: in pursuit of growth for the benefit of everyone: report of the Barking and Dagenham Independent Growth Commission (http://bit.ly/2iT5VFK).

140. G. Kelly. 2015. The debate on social mobility is stuck: time for a city perspective. Gavin Kelly's blog, 18 November (http://bit.ly/2iT5Z8q).

141. S. Marlow, A. Hillmore and P. Ainsworth. 2012. Impacts and costs and benefits of the Future Jobs Fund. Report, Department of Work and Pensions (http://bit.ly/2iT9Keb). For an analysis that counters the claim of government ministers against the FJF, see J. Portes. 2012. The Future Jobs Fund: what a waste. National Institute of Economic and Social Research blog (http://bit.ly/2iTae3l).

142. See the Political Philosophy interview with Jonathan Wolff in 3:AM Magazine on 23 April 2016 (http://bit.ly/2iT5oFr).

143. Speech on the Urban Century given by Tristram Hunt MP at the the People's History Museum, Manchester, 18 April 2016 (http://bit.ly/2hUkLPH).

144. Parker (2015, p. 71).

145. A. Stogia. 2015. Can we make social economy matter in Greater Manchester? New Economy blog, 12 March (http://bit.ly/2hUrxok).

146. Rose (2001, p. 455–64).

147. J. Holden and R. Hewison. 2004. Challenge and change: HLF and cultural value – a report to the Heritage Lottery Fund. Report, Demos (http://bit.ly/2hUwDkH).

148. See, for example, Manchester Camerata's Music in Mind project for people with dementia (http://bit.ly/2hUw8qK).

149. The best starting point for a discussion on the different values of culture is J. Holden. 2004. Capturing cultural value: how culture has become a tool of government policy. Report, Demos (http://bit.ly/2hUkOuu).